June Vigen

MADE FOR MORE
AND
SAVED FOR SOMETHING

MADE FOR MORE
AND
SAVED FOR SOMETHING

MICHELE DAVENPORT

authorHOUSE®

AuthorHouse™
1663 Liberty Drive
Bloomington, IN 47403
www.authorhouse.com
Phone: 1 (800) 839-8640

Published by AuthorHouse 03/28/2017

ISBN: 978-1-5246-8598-0 (sc)
ISBN: 978-1-5246-8596-6 (hc)
ISBN: 978-1-5246-8597-3 (e)

Library of Congress Control Number: 2017904793

Scripture quotations marked NIV are taken from the Holy Bible, New International Version®. NIV®. Copyright © 1973, 1978, 1984 by International Bible Society. Used by permission of Zondervan. All rights reserved. [Biblica]

Print information available on the last page.

This book is printed on acid-free paper.

Contents

Acknowledgements: xi

INTRODUCTION: xv

Chapter One: Palette of Colors 1

Chapter Two: Code Status 8

Chapter Three: War Zone 24

Chapter Four: Keep Walking 42

Chapter Five: Can God Pick a Fight With You? 52

Chapter Six: Pause and Consider This 64

Chapter Seven: Now I Know 74

Chapter Eight: Cold Case Christian 88

Chapter Nine: Spiritual Obesity 101

Chapter Ten: The Good Samaritan 110

Chapter Eleven: Made for More and Saved for Something 118

References: 131

Salvation Prayer 135

"Who I am in Christ" Scriptures: 137

Sample Chapters: *Ripened on the Vine* 143

Sample Poems: *From My Heart to Yours Devotional* 161

Sample Chapter: *Choices are for the Living* 169

YOU WERE

Made for More and Saved for Something!

Realizing your value so you can live in your potential.

Dedication:

I dedicate every word on the pages of this book to my heavenly Father who has taken the time to express His thoughts, wisdom, and knowledge to me. His Spirit was so conspicuous as I was writing. I could literally feel His presence encompassing me, guiding my fingers upon the keys, leading my mind to the thoughts of my Father, and prompting me to express through writing what He wanted to say to His children. I sat, I listened, I typed, and I received revelation that I was made for more and saved for something... as were you.

Acknowledgements:

I would love to give a massive shout out to my Superman. He truly is, beyond a shadow of a doubt, my biggest fan and cheerleader outside of my God. Thank you for allowing me to be all God has called and ordained me to be. Your support over the years has been undeniable. Your authentic love has catapulted me into the woman I'm becoming. I have never experienced such an unconditional love in my entire life. You are truly the real Superman to me because you are a Superman of God, leaping over obstacles, flying through the storms and landing us on the very purpose of God in our lives.

In addition, I would like to dedicate this book to my girls, Whitney Johnston and Dakota Stewart. It has been my privilege to be your mother, and now you are both grown with children on the way. I have gotten to experience your friendship, your love and your wisdom. Thank you for the continual support as I bring the Good News and Vertical Hope to a dying world.

Lori Jonas, my friend and my editor, I want to thank you for all the time you have spent over the years editing my books. You are truly an amazing woman of God whom I admire and esteem. Without you, people would just be reading one long run-on sentence because you know I write exactly the way I talk. I start the book I'm writing, and then I don't put in a period until the end. Ha ha ha ha! I love you so much, lady!

Marco and Erin Hernandez-Reisner, owners and founders of Photos Edge, thank you for accepting the invitation to photograph the cover. You both have photographed some of the most important events in our lives, and this event was no exception. Your gift of catching the right light, the right angle, at the right moment is flawless. Your talent leaves me speechless. What an honor it's been to have you both be part of this experience. I will be forever grateful.

Lastly, I also want to dedicate this book to my step up dad. I had six dads throughout my life, but Robert L. Warren was my step up dad. He died in a tragic drowning accident on October 27, 2016. The best way I can explain what he meant to me is through the poem I wrote him and read at his funeral.

My Step Up Dad

Thank you, Dad, for grafting me in,
For being a father, for being my friend.
You stepped up and took your place,
With so much wisdom, full of grace.
I wasn't born with your eyes or hair,
You never rocked me in a rocking chair.
You didn't hold my hand on the first day of school,
Or sign my reports cards, or teach me house rules.
You weren't there on my first date,
To keep the boy in line or to set him straight.
You entered much later in my life,
But if you ask anyone, you were right on time.
The difference you made by just sowing love,
Changed my perspective on a father's love.
I just wanted to say, you were an answer to prayer,
For a dad to step up and show me he cared.
The trickle effect ran straight down the family line
Because I believe it was your motto, no kid left behind.
I love you, Dad, through the end of time.

What people are saying about…

Made for More and Saved for Something!

Made for More and Saved for Something is a powerfully anointed, must-read for anyone who has ever looked at their life and asked the question "Is this all there is?" Through the use of personal stories, Spirit-led revelation and a unique, new perspective on several familiar Bible characters, Michele leads the reader on a journey to discover the answer. Michele's southern charm, authentic transparency and sense of humor are icing on the cake as she encourages the reader to keep walking into their full potential in Christ. This book is filled with relevant examples and valuable lessons culminating into one simple, yet profound truth… we were ALL *Made for More and Saved for Something*!

Lori Jonas
Women's Ministries
Church of the Harvest, Olathe KS

What an honor for me to review Michele's book, *Made for More and Saved for Something*. The pleasure has surely been all mine. Regardless of what chapter you read, although I highly recommend them all, Michele's character observations are the priceless takeaway throughout this book. It's almost as if Michele had a personal relationship with each one of these Bible personalities. Through her devoted attention and wonderful imagination, my affection for each one has deepened and my interest intensely piqued. It was all I could do not to skip to the last chapter because I couldn't imagine how she could wrap up this amazing gift to her reader; but she did, and she did it gloriously.

Do yourself a huge favor and read EVERY chapter. Fresh. Fresh. Fresh. Each one is a "Faith Builder" and the last chapter is a mammoth payoff of revelation!

My dear, sweet and authentic friend, thank you for your devotion to God and giving Him your hands to type out this wonderful book. I know it will help thousands upon thousands see and understand that they, too, were *Made for More and Saved for Something.*

Jonnie Vitale, Speaker
Pouring Out Hope Ministries
Empower Women's Ministry

INTRODUCTION:

I have ministered to many women who have been abused. They have allowed the abuse to dictate who they are and have determined their value through the eyes of their abuser. No one should have the power or the right to devalue you with their words or actions. You are who God says you are, not what an abuser has tried to diminish you to!

You are worth more than the last encounter with abuse from the abuser. Often times, we don't realize we were made for more because we can't fully comprehend we were saved for something.

Ephesians 2:10, "For we are God's workmanship, created in Christ Jesus to do good works, which God prepared in advance for us to do."

According to the Scripture above, God already has good works for us to accomplish before we even existed. God put into motion a plan and purpose for each one of our lives, but often times through our own decisions, we have found ourselves in the opposite position and direction God wanted us to go.

Why? In my opinion, it's because the value of prayer, and standing still until we hear, has taken a backseat to an impatient spirit with self in the driver's seat, and Jesus in the trunk. We take off with our homemade maps marked with designated pit stops called self, self and one more pit stop for self. All the while, we are headed in a direction we were never meant to go or experience.

Once when traveling to St. Louis to speak at a women's conference at Church in Action, I was on one stretch of road for about three hours. Same road, similar scenery, but the closer I came to my destination, the more I needed to pay attention. There were several exits I needed to take, in addition to being in rush hour traffic, so my eyes were glued to the signs and the road in front of me. I started to slow down so I wouldn't miss my exit. As I was focused on my destination, I heard the Spirit of God say, "You see, Michele, when you know where you're going all the time, you don't pay attention as well. You just go, but did you notice the closer you came to your destination, the more you had to pay attention? You had to slow down, read the signs and look for your exits and yields." I remember thinking, *Yes, Lord, I did notice I had to pay attention more.* He went on to say that's why He does not give us the whole purpose and plan for our lives all at once because we would assume exactly where to go and miss so much of our journey along the way. We would become too familiar and miss the unexpected. We would assume we knew the next step. There would be exits He wanted us to take and yield signs He wanted us to observe, but we would have been too comfortable with the plan and might have missed it all together. There may have been a shortcut, or a detour, or maybe a frontage road He wanted us to take. But again, we would have thought we knew exactly where to go and missed the hand of God in our lives.

It's like this, suppose you and I decide to take a road trip together to one of my favorite destinations. I've been there so many times that I know the route like the back of my hand. We take off and you say, "I know a shortcut." I respond, "Well, I travel this road all the time, I got this." Suddenly we hit a roadblock, a lot of traffic, and an accident. I look at you and say, "I go this way all the time, and I've never run into this much trouble." You look back at me and say, "I knew a shortcut, but because you were so familiar with where you were going, you thought you knew the best way to get us there." So, if I had only been willing to receive direction, we could possibly have saved ourselves a lot of time and trouble.

The same is true spiritually. God has a purpose and a plan for each of our lives, to do good works and finish strong, but for His plan to truly be efficient and effective, we must allow Him the freedom to direct us to our destination. However, we can't get to our destination if we don't take the first step.

You were Made for More and Saved for Something! It's your job and mandate to seek God as to what that looks like in your life.

At the end of each chapter, there will be some discussion questions. I encourage you to answer each question. Write down your first response and meditate on it. Do not overthink it. If you're using the book as a small group Bible study, take this opportunity to discuss your answers aloud and pray for one another. *Made for More and Saved for Something* was created for you to become aware that you truly were saved for something. You have a destination, a purpose, and God has a plan for you. He is in your everyday life. You are not what you do, nor where you've been; you're not even where you are going. You were uniquely designed by God with His purpose for you in mind.

"Before I formed you in the womb I knew you, before you were born I set you apart; I appointed you as a prophet to the nations." Jeremiah 1:5

After I speak at conferences, I always have an altar call. Recently, the Lord told me to start asking one question before praying with an individual. I ask the person I'm praying for to tell me one good thing God has done for them. The reason I do this is to help them remember something God has already done in their lives. It's a Faith Builder. We start with a positive to build on, then we pray on the foundation of faith. So at the end of each chapter, I want you to tell me your Faith Builder for the day, week or month. Follow this with Roadblocks you may have encountered, Exits you took or missed and Yield Signs you acknowledged or flew right through. In addition, write about the Detours you took on your own or were led by God to take. And finally, record your Shortcuts to victory in different situations that appeared during the chapter. This section is called **The Awareness of God's Presence.** Its sole purpose is to make you stop and see how active God is in your everyday life. In the following pages, I will explain what that might look like when you're writing.

*Your Faith Builder is a positive God has done in your life either this week or the week before. Just find something God helped you with, write it down and be aware of His faithfulness.

*The second question is "What was your roadblock this week? What did you experience that you felt like you could not move past?" Stop here and pray alone, or if you're in a small group, pray together about your current situation.

*The third question is "What exits do you think Jesus wanted you to take this week that you either took or missed?"

*The fourth question is "Did you have an opportunity to yield this week?" Following a yield sign is nothing more than taking a purposeful pause in your life to consider and pray about a situation before reacting to it.

*The fifth question is "Did God tell you to take any detours this week?" Meaning, you might have been headed in one direction, but in a moment, He changed your life with an unexpected detour.

*The last question you will answer and discuss after each chapter is "Did God reveal any shortcuts in your life during the week?" Meaning, did He show you, through the Word, any shortcuts to your victory dance?

It's important to observe the road signs in our lives because there are times we will need to yield to God, take an exit, or turn around after hitting a roadblock. Often times, there can be shortcuts on our journey and detours God wants us to make, but if we get too familiar with our surroundings, we may miss an opportunity to stay on the right road.

The second section at the end of each chapter is called **Practical Life Application**. This section is for you to glean from what you learned in the chapter you read. I might ask a few questions, or give you a weekly challenge or both. It's the homework part of the book.

Now let's dive into the deep and swim into the purpose of God in our lives. Allow me to explore some Biblical characters who were *made for more and saved for something.*

Chapter One

Palette of Colors

> *"Do not conform any longer to the pattern of this world, but be transformed by the renewing of your mind. Then you will be able to test and approve what God's will is~~His good, pleasing and perfect will." Romans 12:2*

I shared my horror story to glory story in my first book, *Ripened on the Vine,* which is an account of my life as I was thrust into abuse from a very early age. I survived the first twenty-two years by the grace of God. As death knocked at my door and refused to walk away, I found myself molested when I was eleven at an amusement park in Texas, raped by my uncle, date raped by a boy I trusted, and a victim of a bipolar, heroin addicted mother who was dealing with her own demons as I was dealing with mine. I was held hostage by a drug dealer, who was my step dad at the time, and I was left alone, abandoned to my own devices. I ended up as an alcoholic with a drug addiction for a time . . . BUT God found me in the ditch. He pulled me out, resuscitated my life and washed my sins and the sins of others away. He called me His daughter, clothed me with His righteousness, and made me into a new creation through the blood of His Son and the forgiveness of my sins.

You see, I was born into an entire family line of dysfunction. When my mother gave birth, I became part of the pattern that was begun before me, which in turn, was begun before her, and the one before her... thus starting the pattern of dysfunction.

It's like we're all born with blank canvases. As we grow, people come in and out of our lives, dipping their brush into the paint with which they were painted. Some of those people may have painted some wonderful colors upon your canvas, but some only repeated what was done before them and to them. They flung their abuse, pain and distorted view of power upon your innocence. I call these people "pattern offenders." In other words, they brought their color palette and painted you into the pattern that was created before them. In my life, as I expect in yours at times, it was as if the abusers had a paintbrush, and whatever their past consisted of, then became a part of mine. If they were physically abused, they dipped their brush into the palette of paint and colored me with purple and yellow, the hues of physical abuse. If the abuser was sexually abused, then the brush was dipped into the colors of perversion and flung upon my frail, vulnerable body. If their pattern happened to be verbal abuse, then indeed, they reached for their brush and began to paint me with the graffiti they had been painted with in the years before they knew me. In the same tone they recalled, with the pain of their past in full view, they quickly and abruptly began to destroy my canvas with the words of abuse, each one ripping into the depths of my soul and tearing out a part of me. What once was innocent now damaged at the hand of the abuser, using words as weapons and actions as bullets, while penetrating my heart into the abyss. Mental abuse, which is so often ignored and misunderstood but is still relevant, has its own color. It is distorted by various colors mixed all together forming chaos in the mind of the abuser, thereby leaving the abused confused, emotional, and left stripped of all value as a human being.

"Do not conform to the pattern of this world any longer but be transformed by the renewing of your mind..." (Romans 12:2)

Remember this, because many times we get focused on the colors we were painted, but we fail to realize each one of us holds a paintbrush in our hand as well. Every day, you have the opportunity to paint upon someone else's canvas. Be careful what color wheel you choose to dip your brush in because you will be considered a contributing artist in their lives.

The vertical hope for you today is you can renew your mind. I don't care if great granny, auntie and mamma were drug addicts, you do not have to follow after their pattern any longer. It does not matter if someone painted you their colors, because the truth is Jesus has always been on the sidelines willing and waiting for you to respond to the Master Painter as He creates His masterpiece. He has His own paint palette. His Father gave it to Him as a gift to give to you and me. But you will only see one color on the wheel… the color of white. As He dips His brush and begins to paint upon your tattered canvas, the other colors begin to fade in the background as His love and mercy wash over your life, and the canvas is renewed. In a moment, you are transformed into a new creation in Christ, redeemed for eternity, restored in His likeness. It all happens within that moment you give your life to Christ, but for many, the transformations can take years for our human understanding to grasp the love of the Father. The reason being is many of us, and the number is staggering, have never experienced real love from someone, including a parent.

I struggled for years trying to be someone who was not a victim of abuse. I wanted to be anything besides a victim. I hated the thought of pity and people whispering behind my back things like, "Do you know what happened to her? I heard her family was drug addicts or jail junkies. I heard she was molested at an amusement park, and the park closed while she was still inside with the pedophile. I also heard her dad was a gang member and ended up in prison." "Oh yes, I heard that, but did you hear this? I heard one time, one of her step dads shot his best friend's leg off during a poker game and threw it in a ditch on the way to the emergency room." Or any number of other things people could have said about me.

I just wanted to be normal, with a normal family. I wanted to be made whole. I wanted to live my life in victory, and I was willing to do whatever it took to get me there. Please grab a cup of coffee, a snack if you would like, and follow me into the next chapter as you discover how choosing the right code status can catapult you across the victory line into doing the victory dance with Jesus.

You were made for more and saved for something, but until you realize this one simple concept, you will live beneath your potential. As you journey down your own roads filled with roadblocks, exits, yield signs, detours and shortcuts, allow me to sow seeds of Vertical Hope in your life today.

If you enjoyed this chapter, please subscribe to my YouTube channel where I create three to five minute Vertical Hope videos. Search Michele Davenport with one "L."

Section One: Awareness of God's Presence

Faith Builder----What is something good God has done for you? An answer to prayer, a job opportunity, healing in your body, or maybe a financial breakthrough?

_____

_____

_____

_____

Roadblocks----What roadblocks have presented themselves to you in a positive or negative way? How did you respond?

_____

_____

_____

_____

Exits----Did you see any you needed to take during your week? For example, did you feel God was bidding you to exit a hurtful relationship? Or, maybe God was asking you to take an exit from your current job?

_____

_____

_____

_____

Yield Signs----Were there any situations where you had the opportunity to take a purposeful pause before you reacted to someone or something?

_____

_____

_____

Detours----Did you notice any detours God was trying to take you on? If so, what were they?

_____

_____

_____

_____

Shortcuts----Lastly, many times God will save us from repeating the same mistakes by taking us through a shortcut so we bypass the temptation. Did you recognize God moving like this in your life this week? If so, how?

_____

_____

_____

_____

Section Two: Practical Life Application

Fill in the blank:

"Do not conform any longer to the pattern of this world, but be transformed by the _____ ____ _____ mind..." (Romans 12:2).

How do you renew your mind?

_____

With what color has someone painted you?

_____

With what color have you painted someone else?

_____

Have you forgiven the painter or painters in your life? If not, why?

_____

_____

_____

_____

Read and meditate on Mark 11:24-25. Write your thoughts!

_____

_____

_____

_____

Challenge: If you wrongly painted someone a color they should never have been painted, call, write, or message them with an authentic apology.

Chapter Two

Code Status

"Praise be to the Lord, my Rock, who trains my hands for war and my fingers for battle." Psalm 144:1

It was the winter of 2007 when my husband was sent out of town for a week of training. I was homeschooling our girls, and we had three dogs. One of our dogs was a bird dog named Molly. My husband loved Molly, and he had asked me to keep a good eye on her.

She had a kennel in the backyard with hay and a nice dog house. The week went by without a hitch; it was actually smooth sailing. The day my husband was to return home, I invited another couple over for supper. As I was stirring the meal and preparing the table, I happened to get a glance out of the kitchen window, which was the window that faced our front yard. And there stood the bird dog in all her glory. I walked quietly over to the front door, as if the sound of my walking would disturb her. I gently opened the front door and said in a firm voice, "Molly! Come here!" Again, I said, "Molly!" with a little sterner voice, because I recognized immediately the "ready to bolt" look in her eyes. She looked at me as if to say, "Good luck, lady, I'm out of here. I'm free, I'm free!" And off she ran. Oh my gosh y'all, I grabbed my shoes and started running after her. Within a few seconds, I realized I was no match for her bird dog legs. It was just starting to drizzle snow outside, and the roads were damp and a little slippery. The wind was howling like a wolf in the woods and darkness was covering the sun.

I immediately ran back to my car, jumped in and chased the bird dog up to a country house's winding driveway. I slung the door open, slammed it in park barely in time to jump out, then I proceeded to chase this dog through a stranger's driveway and backyard. I jumped over old railroad ties, weeds, timber, sticks and bushes. Finally, I trapped her on the other side of the barbwire fence. Well, I say I finally trapped her, the truth is I had nothing to do with the barbwire fence that held the bird dog captive, but nonetheless, I was grateful it was there for such a time as this! I walked around the fence, gasping for air, because by this time, I'm in full panic mode and simply out of breath. It was a long driveway and the fence she was caught behind was even farther past the driveway. I was gasping as I got closer and closer to her; I was seeing stars and feeling a little dizzy. I recognized the "ready to bolt" look again in her eyes. I made a split-second decision and lunged at her with my arms sprawled out, and by the miraculous grace of God, they landed right around her neck. What happened next, I cannot tell you. All I know is I came to with my youngest daughter, Dakota, yelling my name, "Mamma, mamma, mamma!" I must have passed out for a moment. I unclenched my arms from Molly's neck; we grabbed her and headed back to the car.

My thoughts were then transported back to the food I left cooking on the stove and the friends who are supposed to be at our house for dinner in a few minutes. We situated Molly, then I ran inside. I had run two miles, at least, and it was sleeting ice at that point. I walked into the kitchen, and by the mercy of my awesome God, my food was not burned. I gave it a stir, then I heard knock, knock. I paused, shook the moment off, and said, "Come in." My friend walked right in and said, "Oh Michele, your hair looks awesome!" *Oh my gosh, really! Is that all it takes to have a good hair day—chasing a bird dog for miles in the snow and sleet and blustering winds?*

A few minutes later, my Superman husband, Marty, came in. Let's pause for a moment, sit up if you're reading this lying down. This may shock you. I've got to be honest, don't judge me. In this moment I'm fixing to share with you, all I wanted was sympathy. That's it, nothing more. I began to tell my husband and my guest what had transpired just before they arrived. I even acted the whole scenario out, with gasping, running in place and diving for Molly's neck as I passed out. I went to great lengths to emphasize the dramatic experience I had. Seriously, after I had reenacted the story, I was sweating and panting again. My husband, my Superman, looked straight at me and said this, "Michele, all you had to do was snap your fingers at Molly and say, 'Kennel up.'"

In disbelief, I responded, "What? Can you repeat that? Can you say it with a straight face? Are you guarding yourself in any way, because I think I might smack you! Let me get this straight. You mean to tell me, I didn't need to put on my Wonder Woman outfit and take off running, hollering, gasping for air, jumping over obstacles and passing out? All I needed to do was look at her and say, 'Molly, kennel up?'" Superman replied, "Yep, that' all."

I pondered this over a matter of days, and it dawned on me that we act the same way with Satan. We are chasing him just like I chased Molly, screaming and hollering, on the verge of hysteria, out of breath and about to pass out, when all we need to do is say, "Satan, kennel up!" You know, he only has the power and authority we are willing to give him. That's all. He has no new tricks. He is the same old devil with the same ol' sack of lies.

"The thief has come to steal, kill, and destroy but I have come that you may have life and have it to the fullest." (John 10:10)

Too many of you are allowing the enemy to put *you* in the kennel where you have accepted the conditions of the evil one.

"What I kept hearing in my spirit for months is "we are living in a war zone." As I sat before the Lord, He started to reveal wisdom to me. He showed me three code statuses of a war zone. This was not your typical war zone. This was a spiritual war zone, a spiritual condition of our lives. For those of you who are reading this book and have a medical background, you will understand the concept well. He showed me the hospital where the wounded were being taken; the hospital was the church. The spiritual code statuses were the conditions of the wounded while enduring the war zone, which represented the world. Everyone who enters a hospital has a code status. For example, a *limited* code status, means if their condition becomes life threatening, you can use some intervention to keep them alive, but you're limited. You can't use all that's available. Then we have the *DNR* code status, which means do not resuscitate. You don't need much of an explanation for this one. If the patient begins to die, don't do anything to keep them alive. Let them die. The last one I'll be sharing is the *full* code status. Again, it's self-explanatory—it means if they are about to die, do everything in your power to keep them alive.

Let's look at the first code status as it applies to the spiritual realm— the *limited* code status. These people want some intervention from the church, but not all, and not at all cost. They may be seeking sympathy rather than wholeness.

"One day Peter and John were going up to the temple at the time of prayer—at three in the afternoon. Now a man who was lame from birth was being carried to the temple gate called Beautiful, where he was put every day to beg from those going into the temple courts. When he saw Peter and John about to enter, he asked them for money. Peter looked straight at him, as did John. Then Peter said, 'Look at us!' So the man gave them his attention, expecting to get something from them. Then Peter said, 'Silver or gold I do not have, but what I do have I give you. In the name of Jesus Christ of Nazareth, walk.' Taking him by the right hand, he helped him up, and instantly the man's feet and ankles became strong. He jumped to his feet and began to walk. Then he went with them into the temple courts, walking and jumping, and praising God. When all the people saw him walking and praising God, they recognized him as the same man who used to sit begging at the temple gate called Beautiful, and they were filled with wonder and amazement at what had happened to him." Acts 3:1-10

The lame man was lame from birth. His condition had become an epidemic in his life. He had a "this is how it's always been, and I guess it's the way it's always going to be" attitude. I noticed after reading the Scripture, the lame man had just enough for the day but never enough to skip a day. In every weather condition, he was brought to the temple gate. If it was pouring down rain, he was there. If it was a hundred degrees outside with a hundred and fifty degree heat index, he was there. If the wind and sand were blowing like a hurricane so that he could not see an inch in front of his face, he was there. If he was sick, he was there. If he had a bad morning, he was there. One thing's for sure, he was dedicated to his condition, to his lameness. It made me ponder the question, *How many of God's blood bought believers are just getting by with enough for the day? How many are dedicated to being lame, broken and dysfunctional?* I also wondered as I was writing, what our lives would look like if we were as dedicated to being whole as we are dedicated to sitting on our mats in the dog kennel, curled up on our hay (where Satan put us)? Saying things like, "If I can just make it through this day. If I can just get the kids off to school, the husband's lunch made, get to work and get busy, I will make it. I won't stop to think about how miserable I am in my marriage. I won't take the pulse of my spiritual condition. No, if I can just make it through this day with little to no change, I'll be okay. It will be alright if I sit outside the temple gate. I've been sitting here for years. I have my favorite spot. My mat fits perfectly. I know almost all the people. I have my favorite tin bucket to collect the sympathy change in. Honestly, I'm quite comfortable in my sickness. At least I know where I'm going when I wake up tomorrow, and what people will expect from me is very little, which is convenient because that's what I'm willing to give."

His friends brought him there every day as they went inside the temple. I noticed also the lame man asked for what he wanted, not for what he needed. This is the epitome of what a limited code spiritual condition looks like. Some of us learn to live with whatever is going on. We become complacent with the sickness, with the depression, with the lack of joy in our lives. We pray like this, "Lord, take the pain," when we should be praying like this, "Lord, heal me, deliver me, restore me. Lord, don't mask the pain; heal the root of the pain."

Watch what God did through Peter and John. He gave the lame man a full code, even though he was content living his life in a limited code status. *"Peter and John said, 'Silver and gold have I none, but what I have I give unto you'."* *Get Up!* Now that's the kind of friends I want in my life. Don't lay me daily at the gate called Beautiful. You better watch out for people who are comfortable leaving you outside the gate every day. They are called enablers.

You might be thinking, *How can someone come into the temple (church) every day and remain the same?* It happens all the time right now in the body of Christ. This man was crippled from birth, but at the time of this story, he was a grown man. He had lived like that for years. Many come to the church every week with the same issues and in the same condition. You know, I was told one time that I don't have a lot of compassion in the normal sense of the word compassion, what they thought compassion looked like. Listen, compassion comes in all forms and ways, and as long as it's rooted and compelled by love, it's compassion. I love you enough not to leave you outside the temple gate. You can cry and tell me how long you've been sitting there, how tired you are of trying to get by. But out of love, I will tell you to pick up your mat and walk. I won't leave you there licking your wounds, and I will not accept the invitation to lick them with you. No, I will say, "Pick up your mat and walk." Pick up what once held you down and carry it to the cross. I will set tools in your hands to help you make it. I will direct you to Jesus, and cheer you on, but, my friend, I won't leave you outside the temple gate. You will need to do the work to be made whole, but I will be by your side to encourage you along the way because you were made for more and saved for something. The lame man outside the gate was settling for his lameness, but you know, when God formed him in his mother's womb, He knew He formed him for more than being lame. His mat became his testimony. He picked up what once held him and testified for Jesus. Why? Because he, too, was made for more and saved for something.

The second condition of the war zone is a spiritual code status called *DNR*-Do Not Resuscitate. Don't do anything to help me. These people come in to church, but nothing really penetrates their hearts. Nothing moves them to change. Nothing grabs their attention for too long. They usually slip in and out of church barely being noticed.

"Do not merely listen to the word, and so deceive yourselves. Do what it says. Anyone who listens to the word but does not do what it says is like someone who looks at his face in a mirror and, after looking at himself, goes away and immediately forgets what he looks like." James 1:22-24

I was talking to a pastor's wife, Denise, one time, and she told me a story about a man who was crippled. Her husband was in seminary, and they lived in an apartment on the second floor, I believe. This is where she met the crippled man. He had to leave his wheelchair at the bottom of the stairs and then crawl up the stairs to his apartment. One day, she decided to ask him if he wanted to be made whole. She said, "Can I pray for you?" He replied, "Yes." As she began to pray for him, the leg that was considerably shorter than the other started to grow back. She would go pray for him often, and the prayers were working. One day, she went to pray for him, and he said, "No." He told her, "I don't want you to pray for me anymore. I don't want to be healed. I get far more attention in the wheelchair than I would if I was healed." Some people are okay with staying on the mat of pity, locked inside a kennel, because they get more attention if there is always something wrong with them. "Oh, look at the poor man sitting inside the kennel." Well, those people have allowed Satan to have the power not only to put them there, but to keep them there.

The code status DNR says, "I'll come to church. I'll smile at you. I'll pretend to be okay. I'll give in the offering. I'll bake a cake for the bake sale. You know, I'll even volunteer for the harvest festival or work the fireworks stand, but don't try to get close to me. I'll slip in and out quietly. I'm spiritually in a drought inside, and I don't want to deal with the real stuff. Do not resuscitate me. I died in the spirit a long time ago." People who live in and with this code status clearly have no idea that they were made for more and saved for something. You were not made to just get by. You were made to thrive!

The last spiritual status code is *full* code. This code means the patient will allow any means to be made whole. Tube me, medicate me, give me CPR, a blood transfusion, or a heart transplant. Whatever it takes to make me whole, just do it. This was me. In the book *Maximized*

Manhood, Ed Cole tells a story about an eight-year-old little girl who was on the list for a heart transplant. I will share the story in my own words.

The waiting was over; the day had come. She was going to get her new heart. Of course, this was bitter sweet, because for her to get a new heart, someone else had to die. Indeed, a ten-year-old little girl was the donor.

A few months after she had received her heart, she started having terrible nightmares. She shared with her mother that in her nightmares, she was being brutally raped and murdered. This went on, each time the little girl giving her mother a little more detail. Her mother was getting very concerned with these nightmares, so she decided to take her daughter to a psychologist.

When she shared the nightmares with the psychologist, she began to describe what the house looked like, and what the room she was being raped and murdered in looked like—the color of the bedspread, the curtains and the boy's face. Immediately, the psychologist turned the information over to the police. The police put all the information together and realized she was describing a teenage boy who was the neighbor of a ten-year-old- girl who was brutally raped, beaten and murdered. He ended up getting convicted for the murder of the ten-year-old who gave her heart to the eight-year-old girl.

Remember when I mentioned a full code person will do whatever it takes to be made whole—CPR, blood transfusion, medication, or even a heart transplant? That is the reason I shared this particular story with y'all. It is a true story. Sometimes in order to be made whole, we need God to remove the nightmares from our heart. We need to forgive some people; we need some people to forgive us. Our hearts need to be figuratively removed and replaced with the heart of the Father, drawn to compassion, filled with grace and mercy, pumping with the blood of Jesus through the arteries of our lives. We need an authentic spiritual heart transplant to become whole.

It will take some work because many of you reading this book today have a heart condition that has gone undetected for so long that you need a triple bypass. Your spiritual arteries have been clogged with the past, some are clogged with un-forgiveness, others are clogged with bitterness, while some have clogged them with the food of this world. You have allowed ambition, love of money, and other fleshly desires to clog your spiritual arteries. You've set goals, achieved goals, set more goals, only to be left empty, lonely and sad. What you thought would bring you joy has only clogged your spiritual arteries. You haven't realized yet, you were made for more and saved for something.

The process for a triple bypass can be lengthy. The surgeon actually has to graft a blood vessel taken from somewhere else in the body to the diseased heart artery, rerouting blood around the blockage in the same way a road detour reroutes traffic around road construction. Many need a rerouting encounter with Jesus. Full code status does whatever it takes to be made whole. Will you?

If asked, I would have considered myself a full code status. Once I received Jesus as my Savior, all I wanted to do was to be a mouthpiece for Jesus. The desire for this deepened with every year until I could no longer be satisfied with telling a few people of His goodness. I needed and wanted to tell millions what He did for me when I was in need of a spiritual heart transplant and how He gave me a blood transfusion using the blood of His Son. I wanted everyone within earshot to hear the good news of how I survived my life for the first twenty-two years. I wanted them to know I was a full code Christian, who was willing to do whatever it took to be whole again. To have my canvas washed with the blood of my Savior and dipped into the palette of paint consisting of only one color, white. As He painted over the sins of others and my own sins, He made me whole.

You know, Superman, a.k.a. my husband, Marty, and I were "tore up from the floor up," but God redeemed, restored, rehabilitated and renewed our purpose for His Glory.

We all need a blood transfusion—Jesus' blood. We all need CPR—the breath of Jesus. We all need a new heart—the heart of the Father. A full code Christian says, "Do whatever it takes. Even if I cry as I walk through the fire, I may feel the heat, but according to God's Word, I will not get burned."

I want to end the chapter with a Biblical example of a woman who I consider a "full code" believer. In *Mark 5:25-34*, we discover an exceptional woman with an issue of blood. She had been suffering with continuous bleeding for twelve years. She was once a wealthy woman who had presence in the community. She may have been on a few committees, probably highly respected, well revered—a noble woman, if you will, but for the last twelve years, she was not even allowed inside the temple. She was considered an outcast. There was no place she fit in or belonged anymore. People didn't even want to be near her, because back then, if you so much as touched someone who was bleeding, you were considered unclean. She was once wealthy but now poor, probably left begging for people scraps. I assume she went hungry many days and had many sleepless, painful nights. She had spent all she had on doctors. She put all her faith in the modern day medicine of the era she was born in. Now broke and even more ill than she had begun, she was an unclean, unwanted outcast who lived only with the other outcast people in the community.

As Jesus was passing by one day, she overheard someone talking about Him. She heard the stories of what He had done. As she leaned in to listen more intently, she thought, *If I can but touch the hem of His clothes, I will be made whole. I will be healed.* Bending down, she began crawling through the crowd where people were almost suffocating to death due to the amount of people surrounding Jesus. She kept whispering, "If I can but touch the hem of His garment, I will be healed. If I can just make it to the hem without being seen or recognized by the others, who would probably stone me to death for defying them and for risking their cleanliness." I can see her in my mind's eye on her hands and knees, inch by inch making her way to Jesus' hem. Repeating, even gasping at times for the words, "If I just touch the hem of His garment, I will be healed." As the dust kicked up from the feet of the travelers, her lungs began to fill with her own saliva mixed with dirt and formed a muddy consistency in her throat.

Barely able to swallow or speak, she opened her mouth one last time, reaching as far as her arms could reach while saying, "If I can but touch the hem of His garment, I will be healed. I will be made whole." In the pure desperation of that moment, her fingers caught the hem, and immediately, her bleeding stopped. She felt in her body that she was freed from her suffering. She was free at last. I envision her dancing in the streets, praising Jesus' name.

In order to receive a complete healing and restoration of your life, you must be willing to become who God created you to be by designating your life to a full code status. Once I discovered who Jesus was, my life changed. I was not who my mamma or my daddy created me to be, but I was the essence of who God created me to be. I realized my life challenges did not define me but gave me an opportunity to live in the realm of a full code status. I was no longer a victim of my past but a survivor of the assault the enemy tried to inflict upon my life. I was healed and made whole by simply choosing to change my code status. Some of you need to upgrade your status because, my friend, you were made for more and saved for something! The most exciting news I have to share with you is now I work for Jesus as a part of the spiritual medical team who has been called to evacuate from our comfort zone and travel into the war zone, dragging out the wounded, so they too can experience the truth that they were made for more and saved for something.

If you enjoyed this chapter, please subscribe to my YouTube channel where I create three to five minute Vertical Hope videos. Search Michele Davenport with one "L."

Section One: Awareness of God's Presence

Faith Builder----What is something good God has done for you? An answer to prayer, a job opportunity, healing in your body, or maybe a financial breakthrough?

_____

_____

_____

_____

Roadblocks----What roadblocks have presented themselves to you in a positive or negative way? How did you respond?

_____

_____

_____

_____

Exits----Did you see any you needed to take during your week? For example, did you feel God was bidding you to exit a hurtful relationship? Or, maybe God was asking you to take an exit from your current job, or from a habit?

_____

_____

_____

_____

Yield Signs----Were there any situations where you had the opportunity to take a purposeful pause before you reacted to someone or something?

_____

_____

_____

_____

Detours----Did you notice any detours God was trying to take you on? If so, what were they?

_____

_____

_____

_____

Shortcuts----Lastly, many times God will save us from repeating the same mistakes by taking us through a shortcut so we bypass the temptation. Did you recognize God moving like this in your life this week? If so, how?

_____

_____

_____

_____

Section Two: Practical Life Application

Praise be to the _____, *my rock, who trains my* _____ *for war and my fingers for* _____.*" Psalm 144:1*

How does God train your hands and fingers for battle? Hint: What do you use to turn the pages of the Bible?

_____

_____

_____

_____

Out of the three different code statuses, Limited code, DNR code, and Full code, which one would you consider yourself in? For your convenience, I've put the definition of each code status below.

_____

_____

_____

_____

Limited code definition:

These people want some intervention from the church, but not all, and not at all cost.

DNR code definition:

These people come into church, but nothing really penetrates their heart. Nothing moves them to change. Nothing grabs their attention for too long. They usually slip in and out church barely being noticed.

Full code definition:

This code means the patient will allow any means to be made whole. "Tube me, medicate me, give me CPR, a blood transfusion, a heart transplant. Whatever it takes to make me whole, just do it."

In our story about the lame man in *Acts 3:1-10*, do you think the lame man could have gotten up and walked before Peter and John showed up?

_____

What do you think happened for him to go from begging and sitting on a mat, to believing and carrying his mat?

_____

_____

_____

_____

What was the one defining moment for the woman with the issue of blood? (*Mark 5:25-34*)

_____

_____

_____

_____

What was the greatest principle you received in this chapter? What ministered to you in the chapter?

_____

_____

_____

_____

Challenge:

If you are not sure what Code Status you are, explain the statuses to someone you trust and ask them which category you fall into. This challenge will take a lot of trust and courage.

Chapter Three

War Zone

*"Finally, be strong in the Lord, and His mighty power.
Put on the full armor of God so you can take your stand
against the **wiles** of the devil. For our struggle is not
against flesh and blood, but against the rulers, against
the authorities, against the powers of this dark world and
against spiritual forces of evil in the heavenly realms.
Therefore, put on the full armor of God so that when the
day of evil comes, you may be able to stand your ground
and after you've done everything, to stand. Stand firm
then, with the belt of truth buckled around your waist, with
the breastplate of righteousness in place, and with your
feet fitted with the readiness that comes from the gospel of
peace. In addition to all of this, take up the shield of faith,
with which you can extinguish all the flaming arrows of
the evil one." Ephesians 6:10-16*

Finally, be strong in the Lord and His mighty power. Not your
husband's power, friend's power, or parent's power, but be strong
in the Lord's mighty power. Why? So you can stand against the
wiles of Satan. "Wiles," in Greek, means "lies in waiting." "Lies in
waiting" means when you go to bed at night, he is busy preparing
his lies—bait, if you will, for when you wake up. He is preparing the
bait that will work on you. I like to fish, but honestly, I don't know a
lot about it. Rarely do I bait my own line, but what I do know from
being married to an avid hunter and fisherman is there's different

bait to catch different fish. For example, to catch a catfish, you might use crawfish as your bait, maybe a minnow to catch a crappie, and tilapia like bright colored bait. You get the picture. What will catch me won't be the same bait Satan uses to catch you.

One morning as my Superman was getting ready to go to the farm to prepare the land for hunting season, he started sharing the process in detail. He told me he had to put salt licks out, check cameras and SD cards, put deer stands in the trees, make sure his camouflage clothes were free of all scent, and practice with his bow and arrow. He went on to say he was conditioning the deer for the kill, stalking them, if you will. My mind immediately went to *Ephesians 6:16... "take up the shield of faith with which you can extinguish all the flaming arrows of the evil one."* This describes Satan to a tee. I preached a message soon after this conversation called *Satan and His Demons Sitting in a Tree.* What a powerful visual I was given on the wiles of Satan.

Three weeks after my mamma died on December 12, 2006, my husband had to leave for training. I was homeschooling the girls. Christmas had come and gone. The tree lights were gently unwrapped from the tree as pine needles fell in a heap on the floor, only to prove it had served us well, and now it was time to be unadorned. The ornaments were slowly taken off as memories flooded my mind with each one. The Christmas CD's no longer playing in the background. The garland and gingerbread men were placed in the box for next year. The last cup of eggnog was waiting to be drunk, and only a few Christmas cookies were left as evidence this holiday had come to a halt. All the lights and festivities had started to fade in the distance as I started to come out of the fog of celebrating Jesus' birthday and mourning my mamma's death.

I had just buried my best friend, and I found myself all alone, desperate for God to heal my broken heart. The pain consumed me; it felt as if it was swallowing me whole and going to digest me slowly. Honestly, I had never felt this kind of brokenness in my life. I had been through my brother's death, my grandma's death, my biological dad's death. I was a survivor of molestation at eleven years old. I endured an uncle raping me with my aunt's approval. I had seen and heard things a child, or an adult, should never have to see or hear. I felt pain before, loneliness before, brokenness before, but not like this, not on this level. I literally thought I was going to die from my broken heart.

At times, I would be walking through the house, and I would literally gasp for air when I was reminded she was gone. I didn't have someone to call mamma anymore. Oh, how I loved her! My agony was indescribable and my sorrow extreme. I longed to sit down with her and tell my mamma about my day, and for her to tell me everything was going to be alright, that I would make it. I longed to hear her laugh just once more, although I can still hear her laugh at times, deep within me. I yearned for her wisdom found and the way she looked at me when she said, "Michele, I love you."

I loved the way she would go over the top when we would come to visit her. My mamma would line the sidewalk with lanterns to welcome us home. Flowers would adorn my room, our favorite foods in the cupboard and ice-box. There was always something cooking on the stove, in case anyone was hungry. The way she lit up when we walked through the door. Oh, the love of a mother cannot be exchanged for any other love. It's unique; it's designed by God.

It's been ten years, and even as I was typing today, I had to pause for a moment to give my heart the space to grieve her absence still in my life. The void I will forever feel. With tears filling my eyes and streaming down my cheeks, I began thanking and praising my God for the time I had with her. Many have had a lot less time with their mammas than I did.

As the dust of that first December settled, although I knew in my spirit I would one day see her again, I couldn't help or deny the emptiness in my soul. The depths of my sorrow ran deep into the soil of despair. The only place I felt like I could breathe was at the feet of Jesus.

Shortly after my husband left for training, the enemy came to my house all dressed up in his hunting gear. It was fifteen days after my mamma was buried in Texas. Here came Satan with his lies in waiting. He showed up with his SD card and camera in hand. He had been watching me, recording me, filming my desperation to get through this season of my life. He indeed brought the bait, along with his weapon of choice—flaming arrows. As he began to play back the video of my pain and loss of my mother, he strategically placed the bait in front of me. He began to whisper his lies in my ears, "You can't make it through this; it's too hard, Michele. She's gone. You will never have her back. Remember the times you got mad at her? Remember when you and your family moved away and how bad that hurt her? You need a drink, Michele. You can't handle this without a drink. No one would blame you or even judge you. You deserve to be out of pain, even if just for a moment. You've been through a lot. Go ahead, get the bottle out." Then he climbed up in his tree stand, pulled back his bow and shot a flaming arrow at my weakness.

As I opened the ice-box, I saw the bottle of cooking wine. I was mesmerized by it, captivated with the endless possibilities, enticed in ways I hadn't been enticed in years. My eyes were fixated on the bottle. I began to entertain and even fantasize about the sweet relief it could bring me. My hands began to sweat, my heart pounded in my chest. I went to grab it from the back of the icebox. Suddenly I stopped and yelled, "No! No! No! *Greater is He who is in me, than he who is in the world.*" I pulled back my hand, slammed the ice-box door and began to cry. I knew it was Satan sitting in his tree stand, waiting to see if he punctured my heart with his flaming arrow. But as the Lord would have it, I ducked, and Satan missed. What once tempted me, no longer had a hold on me. I loved my mamma, and she loved me. There was nothing Satan could say to void this truth. You see, I was made for more and saved for something... and so were you!

This is Satan's M.O. He waits with his lies in his pocket ready to pounce on you. He knew I was a former alcoholic, so that's the bait he chose for me. What will work on me may not work on you. But don't be fooled, he has the right bait for the kill. It's just up to you to quench his fiery darts with the shield of faith, which in Greek, means "truth itself." How do you survive his lies? With truth!

Greater is He who is in me, than he who is in the world (1 John 4:4).

Satan is in his camouflage trying to mask the scent of his presence, but we have the truth which can sniff him out every time. Don't get me wrong, he is an experienced hunter. Some may say he is an expert hunter. He has been hunting since the beginning, starting in the Garden of Eden. I want to use the remainder of my time in this chapter to discuss the five flaming arrows of Satan. They are Doubt, Delay, Defeat, Discouragement and Distraction.

Let's start with Doubt. Doubt certainly has been proven effective in stopping the believer dead in his tracks from accomplishing the will of God in his or her life. I found a real game changer in *Matthew 14:22-32*. Jesus told his disciples to jump in the boat and go across to the other side while He went up the mountain to pray. He sent them into a storm. All of hell was fixing to break loose. Then Jesus showed up during the raging storm, and no one recognized Him. They thought He was a ghost. Before you judge too quickly, this happens now. I've seen it time and time again. People will pray, "Lord help me; send me the answer." Then He does, and because it didn't look the way they thought it should look, they said, "Get behind me, Satan."

When some people read my testimony in my first book, *Ripened on the Vine*, they say, "Where was Jesus, Michele?" My reply is always the same, "Where was He not?" Perspective, my friends, will determine your attitude. You see, you've got to be able to recognize Jesus in your storm. The enemy of our souls would rather us believe we are alone while Jesus remains up on the mountain praying. But no, Jesus came down and met them in the middle of the storm. Peter said, *"If it's You, Jesus, bid me to come."* Listen, this was not after the storm. Nope, this was during the storm while the wind was blowing and the waves were crashing against the boat.

I am held to the belief that Jesus blesses us the most during our storms in life, while we can still see the black clouds and the rain is pounding upon our heads. All the while, the wind is whipping through our hair, and our clothes are still soaked from the downpour. We can still hear the thunder rolling in the background, and witness the lightening splitting the skyline into tiny little pieces. This is when our faith grows. This is when we truly see Jesus. And this is when we grow from glory to glory. What better blessing is there than to grow in faith, see Jesus, and move from glory to glory.

Many people think the blessing is in the absence of trials, but honestly, it was in the trials of my life that I drew closer to Jesus and my faith leapt from mediocre faith to maximized faith. It was in those seasons when I didn't think I was going to make it, Jesus came down from the mountain and rescued me from the raging storm. Satan would have you concentrate on the storm, causing you to doubt and focus on what's happening wrong, instead of focusing on what's happening right. Jesus was in their midst, during the storm.

Peter was the only one who actually got out of the boat during the storm. As his doubt rose up and his eyes centered in on the storm, he began to sink. But we can't deny the man got out of the boat. I know many who are still sitting in the boat, the boat of idleness. The storm has come and gone, but because they fear the next storm, they won't get out of the boat. They are just drifting to and fro waiting for the next big storm, trying to spot the rain cloud.

Let me ask you a practical question. What hurts more people on a boat during a storm? Think about the question, I'll wait. May I say, it's not what's hitting *against* the boat but what's *in* the boat that causes the most damage. How many times have you watched a movie where there's a storm brewing and the captain says, "Tie down the hatch. Secure everything on board. A storm is coming." It's what's in the boat that causes the most damage. I believe when Peter got out of the boat, he left behind eleven others with their doubt, fear, confusion, unbelief, uncertainty, nervousness, faithlessness, cowardliness, hopelessness, helplessness, and blinded to the powerfulness of Jesus. He stepped away from what everyone else was doing. What's in your boat? We will all have storms to endure, but the good news is we can choose how we endure them. You can either keep your eyes on the storm or on Jesus. It's your choice.

The second arrow I want to shine a light on is the arrow of Delay. Most of you know the story of Lazarus being raised from the dead, found in *John 11:1-40*. I want to lay the foundation with some facts. People had been raised from the dead up to three days in the tomb, but never after four. A man named Lazarus was sick. His sisters, Martha and Mary (the same Mary who had poured a year's wages of perfume on Jesus' feet and washed them with her hair), sent word to Jesus that Lazarus was sick. They reminded Him, that Lazarus was the one Jesus loved. Yet when Jesus heard Lazarus was sick, He stayed right where He was for two more days. He spoke with His disciples for a few verses and then told them Lazarus had fallen asleep, but He was going there to wake him up. Of course, the disciples thought Jesus was talking about mere sleep, but He was speaking of death. Jesus said something kind of odd in verses 14-15. He said, *"Lazarus is dead, and for your sake I am glad I was not there, so that you may believe. But let us go to him."* After Jesus arrived, He found out Lazarus had already been dead for four days. When Mary and Martha realized Jesus was in town, Martha said, "Jesus, where were You? If You had been here, my brother would not have died." She went on to say, "No matter what, Jesus, I know if You ask Your Father, He will do what You ask." Martha ran back and told Mary the Teacher was there.

Now, I want to stop here for a minute. Martha and Mary sent word to Jesus saying the one You love is sick, please come. Jesus waited; He did the opposite of what they asked Him to do. While they were waiting for Jesus, their brother Lazarus died. If I was Mary, I may have been like, "Really? Really, Jesus? I poured a year's wages of perfume on Your feet. Not half a year's wages. Not three quarters of a year's wages. No, I poured all of my year's wages upon Your feet. Not only did I pour out an entire year's wages, but I used my own hair to wash Your feet. Now You show up? Now You're here to help my brother? Now that he is dead? After all I did for You, Jesus, You couldn't come back before now?"

This is probably how I might have acted. I bet if truth were told, you might have acted the same way. I know in my early years of being a Christian, I would think, *Well I did this, now it's Your turn to do that. Look Jesus, I tithed this week, so You owe me. I go to church every week, Jesus. Don't You see me putting my check in the box? Now You have to save me from any disappointments.* The sisters did not understand if Jesus knew Lazarus was sick, and He did, why He would delay His appearance. Why would He postpone His visit? Why would He cause such pain if He could prevent it? Because in the delay, laid the miracle. Okay y'all, this was a great place to shout! In the delay, laid the miracle. His delays deserve our praise. The enemy would have you believe the delay is a no, but it can be a yes, disguised in a delay.

My goddaughter, Amanda, used to talk to her mom and me in Fort Worth about her future husband—what his character, personality, and his physical appearance would be like. She wanted someone tall, intelligent and with curly dark hair. As she moved to Missouri, she began to doubt if her Mr. Right was ever going to show up. He did, and right on time, might I add. At their rehearsal dinner, the families played a slide show of the two of them growing up in all different stages of life. As the slide show shuffled through its array of photos, someone noticed Joseph went from straight hair immediately to curly hair. I guess people were asking his mom if he got a perm. She said, "No, he went to bed one night with straight hair and woke up the next morning with curly hair."

At their wedding, I pulled Amanda aside and said, "Remember when you used to wonder if your Mr. Right was ever going to show up?" She said, "Yes." I went on to tell her, "You see, God was putting the finishing touches on your husband. He didn't have curly hair yet, so he couldn't show up until God had finished him for you. So when Joseph laid down one night, God touched his head and dark curls appeared. You see, Amanda, God cares about the details of your life, and He wanted you to have the man of your dreams, including the curly hair."

Satan would try to throw a fiery arrow of delay to discourage you, but God's delays deserve our praise.

The third arrow we will discuss is the arrow of Defeat. Why pray? Why try? Why believe? Defeat waylays more believers than I can tell you. I talk to many people every day who are in the gutter of defeat. They say things like, "I prayed, and it didn't work. I believed and it didn't work. I tried and it didn't work."

Listen, I prayed my grandma would live and not die. She died anyway. I prayed that my mamma would live and not die. She died anyway. I prayed that my brother would live and not die. He died anyway. I prayed my oldest daughter would get pregnant. After 8 IUI's in a row, she is not pregnant. I prayed my youngest daughter's dog would live and not die. She died anyway. We must remember what God has already done for us. It's hard not to feel defeated when you pray, and the answer is not what you wanted or expected to receive. It's hard to understand that my pain is somehow a part of His big painting for my life. It's equally as hard to believe something with all your heart, then it doesn't turn out the way you prayed. It's in these moments we must remember what *Isaiah 55:9* says, *"As the heavens are higher than the earth, so are My ways higher than your ways and My thoughts than your thoughts."* I may not understand all God's decisions in my life, but I will not let them defeat me because I know He knows best in every situation and every scenario in my life. He knows the beginning, middle and end, so therefore, I cannot dispute His infinite wisdom.

Defeat says I have no hope. Elijah sat under a juniper tree asking God to kill him after he had accomplished one of the greatest victories in his life. He called fire down from heaven, but not before he called down rain to pour out on an altar in the middle of a drought. He defeated the 450 prophets of Baal. Then he took off running because a woman name Jezebel started chasing him. He ran straight to the juniper tree and cried out to God, "Just kill me." Why? Why was Elijah begging to die? Because he failed to remember what God had already done in his life. Satan's arrow of defeat works because we have spiritual amnesia. We fail to remember our victories and only remember our battles.

The fourth arrow we will address is the arrow of Discouragement. I can't think of a better Biblical story for discouragement than the story of Abraham and Sarah. In *Genesis 15:5*, God pulled Abraham out of his tent and said, "Look up at the sky. See all the stars? That's how many your offspring will be." Right in the middle of Abraham's discouragement, God showed up with a promise. But first, Abraham had to be willing to look up.

What an exciting time for Abraham and Sarah. But this exciting time in their lives is just verses away from becoming a discouraging, reckless time. When God gave Abraham the promise, he thought it would happen immediately. When it didn't, Sarah became impatient and told Abraham to sleep with her maidservant, Hagar, so the promise would be fulfilled. They substituted God's plan with their plan, and what they ended up with was a human-planned Ishmael, before they received a God-planned Isaac. I've ended up with a few Ishmael's myself, due to impatience and trying to use a substitute plan in place of the real thing. The good news is they learned.

Later, God asked Abraham to sacrifice the promise, Isaac. You don't want to miss this. God told Abraham in *Genesis 22*:2, *"Take Isaac up to a mountain, your only son, Isaac, whom you love, and offer him as a burnt offering to Me. Start walking and I will show you the mountain to go to."* What's amazing to me, and proof that Abraham learned from his mistake with Ishmael, is what he did next. Who did Abraham go get to take up the mountain? That's right, you're getting it; he grabbed Isaac, not Ishmael. Oh, don't you know it would have been easier for him to offer Ishmael? He didn't try this time to substitute the plan of God for his own plan. I really believe the reason Abraham could do this unthinkable thing was because he remembered the prayers God had already answered. He knew the power of God, and he knew that if he sacrificed Isaac, God could bring him back to life. In Abraham and Sarah's discouragement, they gave birth to their plan. In God's mercy and grace, He allowed them to give birth to His plan.

The last arrow I want to share in this chapter is the arrow of Distraction. Let me set the scene for you. Distraction is just another way to say diversion. Have you ever watched a crime show? Did you see how the interrogation room was set up? I've noticed in every crime show I've ever watched, whether innocent or guilty, suspects are always interrogated the same. Because I believe the whole interrogation process is based on the fact that you are considered to be a suspect until you are ruled out.

When preaching this message at my home church, I had an interrogation room set up on the platform, with a spotlight and all… well, it was a floor lamp, but you get the idea! To bring the arrow of distraction home, I used this very powerful visual. I had my event coordinator and friend, Pam, come sit behind the desk as if she was being interrogated by Satan (played by me). All I told her was to say "yes" to everything I asked. That's it. I didn't give her a clue how intense the interrogation was going to get because I wanted an authentic reaction from her and from the ladies who were there that evening. As she walked up, I smiled and told the congregation not to try this at home. This was just a reenactment of a crime. The people's names and identities had been changed to protect the victims. Pam took a seat. Using examples of sins I had heard about through years of ministry, I began to remind her of these things as if they were her past sins. I also mixed in some of my own past sins as part of the scene. Remember this is the final arrow called the ARROW OF DISTRACTION. I believe the Holy Spirit gave me this illustration to shine a light on the truth in a relatable way. So often, we trade the truth for a lie and wonder why we are left feeling defeated and distracted. Okay, sit back and take notes. Here we go.

(**Satan**), "Didn't you apply for a job last week? What makes you think you're going to get it? Didn't you used to do drugs?"

She sat there looking timid and ashamed while shaking her head yes.

(**Satan**) "You think the company is going to hire someone like you—someone who was a drug addict before they hire someone who has never done drugs?"

Her head hung low, discouraged by the enemy's tactics of interrogation.

(**Satan**) "Oh, now that you got your life together, you want to start a family. Do you really think God is going to give you a baby after what you did in 1999? What about that baby? What about his or her life? Didn't you have an abortion?"

She sighed and said, "Yes." Her head fell further down. She was humiliated, sad, and feeling like her life was worthless.

(**Satan**) "Oh, I know you say God forgives, but does He really forgive murder?"

(**Satan thinking**) *Okay, this is working. I'll keep going.*

(**Satan**) "I've heard you cry out to God to deliver you from smoking, but what did you just step outside to do? You don't want to quit; you just want to create lip service to God. You think He is going to honor your prayer? If He were going to help you, wouldn't He have already helped you? If He really cared about you and your health, wouldn't He miraculously heal and deliver you? I mean just take away the desire to smoke. He is punishing you."

(**Still Satan... on a roll now**) "I heard you wanted to write a book. You didn't even finish the 10th grade. You just barely made it through 9th grade, and you were a terrible student. What makes you think you can write a book? You can barely speak English. It's like it's your second language instead of your native language. You were raised by a parent who struggled with heroin. People jumped out of windows at your house. Your home was used to sell drugs out of. People got shot in your house. Who do you think you are to write a book?"

At that moment, I turned to the congregation and smiled because even when he came at me with all his distractions, I went on to write four books... and the fifth one you're reading now.

Throughout the scene, my sweet friend, Pam, was acting the part we have all been guilty of playing. She had given ear to the enemy and never fought back. At this point, it was time to bring the scene to an end. I reminded the audience that this was a dramatization, and I thanked my dear friend, Pam, for being such a good sport. Because she knew she could trust me, she played along and portrayed an all too common response to the attacks of Satan. Now, I know Pam well, and I know her to be a mighty woman of God who is not unaware of the schemes of the devil. It is because of her strength in the Lord and her ability to stand on the Word of God that I knew she could handle being a part of this visual example of a spiritual truth.

You see, *Satan is a liar, the father of all lies* is what the Word of God says. He can't do anything but lie. You want to know how Satan gets in? It's through his lies. He loves to isolate and intimidate us with half-truths. For example, you may have had an abortion at one point in your life, but *Psalm 103:12 says, "...as far as the east is from the west, so far has he removed our transgressions from us."* Have you ever wondered why God used east and west instead of north and south? Well, it's because if you travel north long enough, you will eventually have to go south if you continue traveling. The same is true of traveling south long enough—eventually, you would have to go north to continue. North and south meet at the poles, or in other words, they cross each other. However, if you travel in one continuous direction going either east or west, you are never forced to go in the opposite direction. East and west never meet; they never cross. They are as far removed from each other as any measurable means. God was essentially saying, "I forgive you and the memory of that sin will never run across My mind again. It is forgotten!" Maybe you did drugs in the past, but the Word of God says, *"Therefore, if anyone is in Christ, the new creation has come: The old has gone, the new is here" (2 Cor. 5:17)!* Are you beginning to see how to fight back when Satan is firing his darts, especially those of distractions from your past? He fights his battles with lies, you fight yours with the truth of God's Word—it's your sword.

It does not matter what you used to do, because once you gave your life to Christ, you became *a new creation. All things old are gone, the new is here.* Your past can never change who you are in Christ today. Yaymen!

Satan has no new techniques and no new lies. *He is just roaming around looking for someone to devour.* The question is will he find you? Are you easy prey for the enemy? Let's take a stand and refuse to bow down to the enemy's tactics, because you were made for more and saved for something. So let's live like it!

If you enjoyed this chapter, please subscribe to my YouTube channel where I create three to five minute Vertical Hope videos. Search Michele Davenport with one "L."

Section One: Awareness of God's Presence

Faith Builder----What is something good God has done for you? An answer to prayer, a job opportunity, healing in your body, or maybe a financial breakthrough?

_____

_____

_____

_____

Roadblocks----What roadblocks have presented themselves to you in a positive or negative way? How did you respond?

_____

_____

_____

_____

Exits----Did you see any you needed to take during your week? Like for example, did you feel God was bidding you to exit a hurtful relationship? Or, maybe God was asking you to take an exit from your current job.

_____

_____

_____

Yield Signs----Were there any situations where you had the opportunity to take a purposeful pause before you reacted to someone or something?

_____

_____

_____

Detours----Did you notice any detours God was trying to take you on? If so, what were they?

_____

_____

_____

_____

Shortcuts----Lastly, many times God will save us from repeating the same mistakes by taking us through a shortcut so we bypass the temptation. Did you recognize God moving like this in your life this week? If so, how?

_____

_____

_____

_____

Section Two: Practical Life Application

Fill in the blanks:

In addition to all of this, take up the shield of _____, with which you can extinguish all the flaming _____ of the _____ one." Ephesians 6:16

As we have studied throughout the chapter, there are five flaming arrows Satan uses on the believer. The arrow of Doubt can make you stumble so quickly if you are not rooted deep in the Word of God. As the storm approached the disciples, Peter was the only one who decided to do something. He cast doubt aside and jumped into the deep with Jesus. During your last storm, what is something you did that left others still sitting in the boat of doubt?

_____

_____

_____

_____

If you can't think of an example, maybe you stayed in the boat... maybe you're still tucked away safe in the boat. Jesus came down off the mountain during their storm, but they did not recognize Him. Do you?

_____

The arrow of Delay is the second arrow we discussed. His delays deserve our praise. In the framework of that statement, when was the last time you were in a circumstance that caused a delay to your prayers?

_____

_____

Did His delays deserve your praise?

_____

The arrow of Defeat is our next arrow. Elijah had just had one of his greatest victories, yet he sat under a juniper tree begging God to kill him. Why? Because he felt defeated. He felt defeated because he failed to remember his victories. So with that being said, write down a victory you have had with God in the last week.

_____

_____

_____

_____

The fourth arrow we studied was Discouragement. The example given was with Abraham and Sarah after God told them they would have a son. Instead of standing on the promise, they decided the promise was taking too long and took matters into their own hands.

Sarah told Abraham to sleep with her maidservant, Hagar, which in turn, gave them an Ishmael.

Have you ever given birth to an Ishmael because you tried your plan instead of trusting God's plan? _____ If so, what was it?

_____

_____

_____

_____

Distraction is the last arrow we studied. Have you ever felt like you were in the interrogation room with the enemy? _____ Has he ever made you feel like God was not going to answer your prayers because of something you did in the past?_____ What Scriptures did you stand on to strengthen yourself in the Word?

_____

_____

What piece of armor do you consider to be the most important piece to put on and why?

_____

_____

_____

_____

Chapter Four

Keep Walking

"Now Jericho [a fenced town with high walls] was tightly closed because of the Israelites; no one went out or came in. And the Lord said to Joshua, See, I have given Jericho, its king and mighty men of valor, into your hands. You shall march around the enclosure, all the men of war going around the city once. This you shall do for six days. And seven priests shall bear before the ark seven trumpets of rams' horns; and on the seventh day you shall march around the enclosure seven times and the priests shall blow the trumpets. When they make a long blast with the rams' horn and you hear the sound of the trumpet, all the people shall shout with a great shout; and the wall of the enclosure shall fall down in its place and the people shall go up [over it], every man straight before him." Joshua 6:1-5 (Amplified)

The impala is a fascinating animal out of eastern and southern Africa. It's a medium-sized antelope. The impala can leap up to 30 feet in distance and jump as high as 10 feet vertically. The information that I found most interesting after reading about the impala was it could be kept behind a three foot wall at the zoo. Why, you may ask? Because an impala will not jump if he can't visualize where he will land. To be honest, during my years of ministry, I have met many who have an "impala spirit." They will not take a leap of faith because they can't see where they will land. Sometimes, as frustrating as it can be, God wants us to jump before He starts to fill the pool.

The Lord told the Israelites to take off and keep walking. He told Joshua to take the Israelite army, and seven priests with seven trumpets of rams' horns, and hike around Jericho for seven days. On the seventh day, they were to march around the city seven times and then stop and shout. We don't want to miss the number seven and its significance here. The number seven represents the covenant between God and Israel. It's a symbol of completeness. What God promised Abraham generations earlier concerning the Promised Land, He was fixing to complete. Hebrew letters are also assigned a number and a picture. The Hebrew language is very poetic. The number seven is the word *Zay-een*, and it's a picture of Jesus. Jericho was the oldest city in the world. It was about eight to nine acres in size. God came to Joshua and told him His big plan to take down a fortified city with walls that were thirty feet tall, twenty feet deep and consisted of two layers... and Joshua shared the vision.

You see, Israel had been landless for about fifty years. They were ready to take the Promised Land. What sounds ridiculous to us was God's plan for them to win the battle. As I was studying the story, I realized there are three possible reasons we stop walking toward our Promised Land filled with milk and honey, which essentially means "God's spiritual best."

The first reason is we can't see over the three-foot wall. Let me tell you, just because you can't see the promise does not mean it isn't there. Remember, I told you the walls were thirty feet high. They could not see the land from where they stood. A fortified wall does not forfeit God's promises. You know, when God told me to write my testimony in my first book, *Ripened on the Vine,* I thought, *I can barely speak English correctly and now You want me to write it?* I didn't even finish the tenth grade, and English was my worst subject. Well let's face it, I'm not sure I had a best subject! Although I could not see over the three-foot wall, I did have faith enough to jump before God started filling the pool. I knew I couldn't do it, but I knew God could. I'm so glad I did because *Ripened on the Vine* is in the prisons all over the United States as well as in Nancy Alcorn's Mercy Ministries' libraries around the world.

This one book has helped hundreds and hundreds, if not thousands of people, find their voice and walk out forgiveness in their own lives. Keep walking because you were made for more and saved for something.

One day, I was sitting in a salon with my daughter getting my hair done. There was a very unusual lady sitting catty-corner from me. I thought she might have gone through something; she seemed out of sorts. Her hair was very short and was all wrapped up in foils. She had a lot to say to anyone who would listen. Her language was colorful, and her personality was distracting. She began a conversation with me, then within minutes, whipped out some photographs of her missing breast. She began to share her story of breast cancer. Everyone around us seemed to be a little disengaged with her. She was loud, talked a bit like a sailor and was very abrupt. As she was sharing, I began to see the wounded woman she was. My hair was done; time to go, but before I did, I felt the Holy Spirit telling me to go pray for her. My daughter started walking towards the door. I walked over to the lady instead and began to pray healing over her body, peace over her mind, wisdom in her upcoming decisions, and the love of the Lord in her life. I handed her a card and told her to get my book. She looked at me and said in the sweetest, smallest voice, "Thank you, you just made my day." She was also made for more and saved for something. She was more than the cancer, and she was saved not just to survive, but to thrive, on her journey.

You know, it's moments like those that I'm glad I have this ability to jump before I can see where I will land. For all I knew, she could have cussed me out and punched me in the nose, but instead, she embraced the God in me.

The second reason I believe we stop walking toward our Promised Land filled with God's spiritual best is . . . we don't see any change, or any evidence of change, in our situation.

You know, the Israelites walked around Jericho every day for six days in silence. It was only a thirty minute walk around, so for the next twenty three and a half hours, they were left with their thoughts. I didn't read there was a lot of murmuring going on. As a matter of fact, I didn't read there was any murmuring going on at all. I believe they were fighting their battle with the promise in sight.

I'm just going to be straight up honest with you. If this would have been me, and it has been on many occasions, I'm the type of person who would have walked around once, and then I would have wanted God to say, "Good job, Michele! Since you did not complain, I'll shave five minutes off your time. Keep walking!" If I walked around twice, I would have wanted God to say, "Oh, Michele! You did a great job again being obedient and staying the course. Let me get you a treat." You see y'all, I'm motivated by progress. That's why I like to paint stuff because I get to see results fast. You know, I want to see a crack in the Jericho wall or some evidence that the wall is coming down, like maybe each time I walked around, a brick or two would fall. But, no! This was not how it worked for those seven days. They walked around for six days not saying a peep, with no evidence that what God told them to do was going to work. There was no crack in the wall, no bricks hitting the ground stirring up the dirt so they could get a glimpse of some real tangible evidence the plan was working. I'm so motivated by progress that I make a list so I can mark stuff off the list. And if I dare do something that's not on my list, I write it on the list just so I can mark it off!

If everything stays the same after God said you were going to get promoted to a higher position, keep walking. If your ministry stays the same after you received a word it was going to flourish, keep walking. If your prayers seem to fall on deaf ears, keep walking. God is always doing more behind your back than in front of your face. If you gain thirty pounds after going through early menopause at the tender age of 36, then keep walking. Literally! I was the only person I knew who could go on a two mile run, come back and gain two pounds! Ten years it took me to lose thirty pounds. Keep walking. I remember when we lived in Omaha, Nebraska. It was a cold night, and I thought after the girls went to bed, I would try to be sexy. I put on a little somethin' somethin' and started down the stairs. I thought I would take a glance back to our bedroom and strike a pose at the handrail of the stair case. As I went to put my hand on the rail, I missed it all together and fell down the stairs. Oh my, I may look the part, but I can't act the part. Get up and keep walking!

The last thing that keeps us from walking in our Promised Land filled with God's spiritual best is lack of obedience. *"Obedience is better than sacrifice" (1 Samuel 15:22).* Can you imagine if Noah said, "I can't see the rain. I'll build the ark when I can see the first raindrop." When God told Ezekiel to speak to the dry bones, what if Ezekiel would have said, "I'll wait until the bones come alive so I don't look stupid talking to dead bones." There is a powerful lesson in Ezekiel 37. What once was dead, when spoken to with the authority of Jesus, can be brought back to life. What a wonderful picture of our spiritual life. The woman with the issue of blood, she kept walking and touched the hem of Jesus' garment. And she was healed of a twelve-year sickness.

What about Moses? What if he hadn't been obedient and gone to speak to Pharaoh? The Israelites might still be in bondage. Joshua crossed the swollen Jordan during flood season, because he chose to obey and have the priest put a toe in the river. *Then* it parted, so they could cross over. Keep walking. The same goes with Moses and the Red sea. God told him to lift his staff and the sea would part. If Moses hadn't been obedient, they would have all been taken back to Egypt and placed in bondage once again. What if Jesus didn't keep walking to the cross? God provided our salvation because Jesus kept walking. How about Abraham when he went up the mountain to sacrifice Isaac? God provided because Abraham kept walking. Sometimes, we don't see our miracle because we refuse to keep walking. Job lost everything, but he kept walking. Then, he said in *Job 42:5, "My ears had heard of You but now I see You."* He said this after he lost everything.

Some of the stuff God had people doing looked ridiculous to the naked eye, but one thing it ensured—God received all the glory. Disobedience will keep you out of your Promised Land. You must keep walking in order for the walls to come down. You may not be able to see over them. You may not have one piece of evidence to prove they are indeed coming down, but obey anyway, keep walking anyway, because the God of the universe can bring any wall down. If the doctors say you have a lump in your breast, keep walking. I did! When they went back to confirm the lump and do a biopsy, it was gone. When the doctor says your child has the blood of a dying child, keep walking. I did! The final verdict of the doctor was "unexplained blood." No, I can explain it. She has the blood of Christ running through her veins! She is healthy and well to this day. When the school says your youngest child will never read past a second grade level, keep walking. I did! I homeschooled her, and now she is a CNA.

Listen, don't stop walking because you may be on your last lap. The trumpets are about to blow, the victory shout is about to come. When nothing changes, keep walking, because you were made for more and saved for something. Yaymen!

If you enjoyed this chapter, please subscribe to my YouTube channel where I create three to five minute Vertical Hope videos. Search Michele Davenport with one "L."

Section One: Awareness of God's Presence

Faith Builder----What is something good God has done for you? An answer to prayer, a job opportunity, healing in your body, or maybe a financial breakthrough?

_____

_____

_____

_____

Roadblocks----What roadblocks have presented themselves to you in a positive or negative way? How did you respond?

_____

_____

_____

_____

Exits----Did you see any you needed to take during your week? For example, did you feel God was bidding you to exit a hurtful relationship? Or, maybe God was asking you to take an exit from your current job, or from a habit?

_____

_____

_____

_____

Yield Signs----Were there any situations where you had the opportunity to take a purposeful pause before you reacted to someone or something?

_____

_____

_____

_____

Detours----Did you notice any detours God was trying to take you on? If so, what were they?

_____

_____

_____

_____

Shortcuts----Lastly, many times God will save us from repeating the same mistakes by taking us through a shortcut so we bypass the temptation. Did you recognize God moving like this in your life this week? If so, how?

_____

_____

_____

_____

Section Two: Practical Life Application

Fill in the blanks:

"When they make a long blast with the rams' horn and you hear the sound of the _____, all the people shall shout with a great _____; and the wall of the _____ shall fall down in its place and the people shall go up over it, every man straight before him." Joshua 6:5 (Amplified)

The Israelites were told to march around Jericho seven times on the seventh day with seven priests and seven trumpets of rams' horns. Then on the seventh lap, they were to blow the horns, and the walls of Jericho would come down. What was the importance of the number seven?

_____

_____

_____

_____

What keeps the African impala behind a three foot wall?

_____

_____

_____

_____

What has kept you behind a three foot wall?

_____

_____

_____

_____

Name the three things I mentioned that could keep you out of your Promised Land.

1._____

2._____

3._____

Have any of the scenarios I mentioned in this chapter kept you from your promise? How?

_____

_____

_____

_____

Chapter Five

Can God Pick a Fight With You?

"That night Jacob got up and took his two wives, his two maidservants, and his eleven sons and crossed the ford of the Jabbok. After he had sent them across the stream, he sent over all his possessions. So Jacob was left alone, and a man wrestled with him until daybreak. When the man saw he could not overpower him, he touched the socket of Jacob's hip so that his hip was wrenched as he wrestled with the man. Then the man said, 'Let me go, for it is daybreak.' But Jacob replied, 'I will not let you go unless you bless me.' The man asked him, 'What is your name?' 'Jacob,' he answered. Then the man said, 'Your name will no longer be Jacob, but Israel, because you have struggled with God and with man and have overcome.'" Genesis 32:22-28

What happens when God allows you to be broken? Or even, when He's the One who breaks you? Have you ever been in a fight with God where you felt like He was picking on you? You felt like He was your big brother, instead of your heavenly Father. If you think about it, God can stop anything, but often times, He allows it. Why? Honestly, I don't know. All I know is He does allow it, because He can stop it. What I do completely understand is God has given us a free will to choose right or wrong. He didn't create robots. In the garden on one tragic afternoon, we chose to eat from the forbidden tree, letting all the knowledge of good and evil enter our atmosphere. As we stood with fig leaves covering our once unashamed naked frames, God showed up calling out to His children, "Where are you?" We are over here, and we are afraid because we made the wrong choice. God placed His punishment upon them along with the evil serpent. They were cast out of the perfect garden with the perfect life, where no sin prevailed and no moments of sadness overtook their joy. It was in this atmosphere that Adam and Eve chose to eat from the forbidden fruit, and sin, ushered into our perfect world, propped its feet up on righteousness and laughed. But the day would arrive that God would supply us His only Son, who bore the name of Jesus, to die for our sins and restore us to right standing with Him once again.

So with this knowledge, I understand bad things happen to good people because we have all been given free will to choose right or wrong. And for some, the decision to choose badly is the easy one to make.

Looking back on my own life and experiences, sometimes I had to walk through the Red Sea, instead of around it, because the lesson I learned walking through it far outweighed any benefit of being spared from the experience. Sometimes it's more important that God builds our faith rather than giving us what we want immediately. There is something in believing against all odds that God will show up on our behalf. I call these moments *faith builders.*

God allowed Joseph to be sold into slavery, but Joseph learned how to rule and stay faithful to God. God allowed Job to be tempted by Satan; He even suggested it. But after it was all over, when all had been lost, when Job had buried all his children, oxen, cattle and donkeys, when his friends had turned against him and his wife said, "Why don't you just curse God and die," it's then, in the last chapter of *Job, chapter 42,* Job says these famous words, *"My ears have heard of you, but now my eyes have seen you."* What? You mean to tell me after Job had gone through the fire, through the grief, through the pain, through the loss and humiliation, he said those words?

Job learned how to truly see God's heart, power and authority. The whole experience brought Job closer to God and helped him believe he, too, was made for more and saved for something.

God told Noah to build an ark on dry ground, which he did for 120 years, all the while being mocked and ridiculed. But Noah learned obedience through the trial. God saved him and his whole family, because they were made for more and saved for something besides drowning in the huge flood.

Before I can take you where I'm going, I have to catch you up to where I am in my mind. I've already shared with you earlier about how Abraham was promised a son in the book of Genesis. It was taking too long so Sarah, Abraham's wife, told Abraham to sleep with her maidservant, Hagar. Hagar became pregnant and gave birth to their human-planned Ishmael. But finally, they were able to get ahold of God's promise and timing for the birth of their promised child. In time, Sarah gave birth to the God-planned Isaac. Isaac married a woman named Rebecca; they had two sons, Esau and Jacob. The brothers were at war; even in the womb, they fought. Rebecca asked God why her children were fighting. He said she had two nations fighting inside her. The youngest would rule over the oldest. When the twin boys decided to make their appearance, Jacob came out holding onto the heel of Esau. Esau was a warrior, a hunter. The Bible says he was a hairy man. Jacob was a mamma's boy who hung out around the tent. One day, Esau came in from hunting, and he was starving. Jacob offered him some stew. Esau jumped at it, but then Jacob said, "I'll give you some stew for your birthright." So Esau gave Jacob his birthright while chowing down on the bowl of stew.

Jacob deceived Esau. Later, Isaac, their father was on his death bed fixing to die. His eyesight was gone, his body frail, his mind slipping, his age showing on his face—the wrinkles told the story of a man who was born as a promise. His hands shook beneath the covers, his lips dry as he whispered the name of his firstborn son, Esau. He bid Esau to his bedside to give him the first son's birthright blessing. Isaac told Esau to go hunting and kill something to eat. Then he was to prepare a meal for Isaac and Isaac would pass the blessing on to him. Rebecca, Isaac's wife, overheard the conversation and sent Jacob, her favorite son, to their dad's bedside to deceive him. Rebecca put hair all over Jacob's arms and sent Jacob in with a meal. Unknowingly, Isaac passed down the first son's birthright blessing to Jacob.

You don't want to miss this teaching moment. Remember what God told Rebecca when she asked why her sons were fighting in the womb? God said that Jacob, the youngest, would rule over the oldest. Rebecca took the information God gave her and tried to make that happen on her own, just like Sarah tried to work out the promise of Isaac on her own and ended up with Ishmael.

It was a done deal now. Jacob had received the firstborn blessing rights. After Esau finished hunting, he came running in with some food and ready for the blessing. He soon realized what had happened, and he declared if it was the last thing he did, he was going to kill his brother. Rebecca realized Jacob was in serious trouble, so she sent him off to her brother, Laban's, to live.

A lot happened between the pages of *Genesis chapters 28-32*. But for the sake of trying to catch you up to where my thoughts are still waiting, let's keep moving. Jacob lived with Laban and took two wives that he worked for for fourteen years. One night, he decided he was tired of Laban, and he took off with his wives and children. The Bible called Jacob a deceiver, which again proved true because he deceived Laban. Jacob headed back to Canaan and sent an offering ahead of him to appease Esau. Esau sent four hundred men to meet Jacob; he was still hanging onto some un-forgiveness.

Jacob sent everything and everyone across the stream; at that point, he was completely alone. Now we have caught up to my thoughts, praise the Lord!

"That night Jacob got up and took his two wives, his two maidservants, and his eleven sons and crossed the ford of the Jabbok. After he had sent them across the stream, he sent over all his possessions. So Jacob was left alone, and a man wrestled with him until daybreak.

When the man saw he could not overpower him, he touched the socket of Jacob's hip so that his hip was wrenched as he wrestled with the man. Then the man said, 'Let me go, for it is daybreak.' But Jacob replied, 'I will not let you go unless you bless me.' The man asked him, 'What is your name?' 'Jacob,' he answered. Then the man said, 'Your name will no longer be Jacob, but Israel, because you have struggled with God and with man and have overcome'" Genesis 32:22-28.

Watch this… God showed up in human form and picked a little fight with Jacob. We are not used to taking a peek at the Scripture like this. It might even make us feel somewhat uncomfortable. We are used to reading how *"our walls are ever before him and our name is written on the palm of his hands" (Isaiah 49:16)*. We like reading how God *"sent a cloud by day and fire by night" (Exodus 13:21)*. Or how *"God held the sun and the moon still until Israelites defeated their enemies" (Joshua 10:13)*. Oh, we love the God of the rainbow, but what about the God who brought the hugest flood this world has ever seen to date? What about all those children who died? What about all the people who drowned? The animals that were killed? We miss the God who allows pain for a moment if it brings about a restored outcome in the end.

I remember when I was trying to get pregnant. We were newly married with our whole lives before us. The day came when we decided to start a family. Six months had passed and no baby. We decided to have Marty checked. He was okay. Then we checked me. I needed to have my tubes blown out, other than that, I looked good. We kept trying but to no avail. Months turned into years. I cried out every month, "Why, God, why?" I felt isolated and alone, and to make matters worse, my mamma and my step up dad had to move to Florida for a year for my dad's job.

We kept trying; the pain of seeing all my friends getting pregnant was overwhelming at times. We sought after God, we prayed, we believed, but nothing. I started dressing my dog in clothes. I wanted a baby. That's all I could focus on. I mean seriously, I almost stuck a pacifier in my dog's mouth! The pain was unbearable at times, more than I thought I could handle.

A year had passed, and it was finally time for my mamma and dad to move back to Warsaw from Florida. That weekend, I was driving down to see them, and I felt like I was pregnant. That wasn't unusual though, I felt like I was pregnant every month. After I arrived, I announced, "I think I'm pregnant" and asked if we could go to the clinic the next day so I could take a pregnancy test. My mamma said, "Sure." The next morning, we got up and headed to the clinic. I did all the things they asked me to do and then sat outside the little waiting area with my mamma. When I heard them call, "Michele," I went into the examination room, and I was told I was pregnant. Listen, God's timing is perfect, although I could not see it while I was going through the trial. Had I gotten pregnant when I wanted to, my mamma would have missed so much of the journey. I was her only child left, and God not only cared about my prayer request, He cared about my mamma's as well. I learned some valuable lessons during my season of waiting for God's perfect timing in my life to bear a child. Many of us want a mountaintop experience, but we don't want to go through any valleys. I went through the valley, but I'm here to tell you the view from the mountaintop was so much more refreshing because I walked through some valleys to get there.

We tend to forget the God of Isaiah. "...*My ways are higher than your ways and my thoughts are higher than your thoughts" (Isaiah 55:9).*

A God who showed up to pick a little fight with Jacob. Who would think this? But honestly, this was God too. In *verse 25*, God began to wrestle with Jacob. He picked a fight He couldn't win, so God broke Jacob's hip. Stay with me—don't close the book yet. There is truth here. I know you prefer the God who heals the blind... me too. Makes the mute speak... me too. Opens the deaf ears, heals the lepers, parts the Red Sea... me too, me too, me too, but this is God also. This may feel very uncomfortable for you, and quite frankly, it is for me as well. But if God can prevent it, and we know He can, then there is a reason He allows it. Can we agree on that? Ask yourself this one question,

"What kind of battle can I be in with God that He can't prevail?" What battle is in your life, in my life, that God cannot win?

The answer is quite simple, the battle of our free will! Our Flesh! Jacob was suffering from an identity crisis. He came from a line of deceivers. He was following the pattern which was painted before him. Rebecca knew the youngest was going to rule over the oldest; God had told her. I don't have any proof, but there must have been some kind of talk about the youngest ruling over the oldest. Maybe Rebecca shared with Jacob when he got older what God had told her. Maybe this was why Jacob didn't get his hands dirty very often. Maybe he thought, *I'm going to rule over my brother. He can hunt and slave for our food, but I'm going to wait for the day I rule.* I can imagine Rebecca having talks with her favorite son, Jacob, telling him all about how he was going to get the firstborn birthright, as if she was grooming him for the very moment Esau came running into the camp, starving. "Sure I'll feed you, but give me your birthright first." In other words, let me make this promise come to pass. Sound familiar? It should; it's exactly what Abraham and Sarah did when they substituted their plan for God's. Remember? They ended up with a human-planned Ishmael, before they had the God-planned Isaac. Now Isaac's son, Jacob, was repeating the same pattern.

In *Genesis 32:26* though, after the breaking, Jacob was just holding onto God. He was no longer fighting Him. It's in the brokenness we learn how to hold onto God. I lost my whole family, and in the brokenness, I learned how to hold onto God. If God loved you enough to allow His only Son to die for you, He loves you enough to break you. If there is a break, you can bet there is going to be a blessing somewhere.

God said to Jacob, "What is your name?" Jacob answered, "Jacob," which in a way was his confession. God said, "I don't like that name. It means deceiver, a con man, if you will. Your name is now Israel." Listen y'all, God broke Jacob to birth Israel! You don't want to miss this—God may be breaking something in you to give birth to something through you. Oh, I don't think you read this right because I didn't hear the book drop and hit the floor! You see you can't stay the same after an encounter with God, because you were made for more and saved for something. After wrestling with God, Jacob could no longer be a deceiver, he had to be an Israel. Why? Because Jacob was made for more and saved for something.

When my first book, *Ripened on the Vine,* was published, my name was spelled with one L on the outside of the book, but on the inside, it was spelled with two L's. It really bothered me. Then God spoke to me. He said, "Michele with one L, the Michelle with two L's on the inside of that book is not who you are anymore." That's exciting! I didn't even know my name was spelled with only one L until I was in my mid-thirties, and by then, I sure was not the same old Michelle with two L's! I was blind, but now I see. I was broken, but now I'm mended. I was sick, but now I am well. I was a victim, but now I am victorious. I was lost, but now I am found. Oh, how I love my God! God allowed the breaking, but a blessing came from it all. I was broken, but there was a blessing. I was then allowed to break a few things myself. I broke off the pattern of addiction in my life. I broke off divorce, abuse, abandonment, mental illness and depression. There is a blessing in the breaking.

God broke Jacob to give birth to Israel. Don't form your opinions and gossip about others who are going through their own breaking moment, because God is birthing something in them that could not have been birthed without the birthing process. You know when you actually give birth, the baby has to break through the skin to be born. There is a blessing in the breaking process; ask any mamma who has given birth.

God said I'm going to call you Israel because you wrestled with God and man and prevailed. You might be thinking Jacob did not prevail. You're right, Israel did! Israel prevailed over Jacob the deceiver. It's a little ironic that the name Israel means *"may God prevail."* Just like Sarah prevailed over Sarai, Abraham prevailed over Abram, Paul over Saul and Michele with one L over Michelle with two L's, you were made for more and saved for something. Don't reject the breaking because God is trying to birth a blessing through it.

If you enjoyed this chapter, please subscribe to my YouTube channel where I create three to five minute Vertical Hope videos. Search Michele Davenport with one "L."

Section One: Awareness of God's Presence

Faith Builder----What is something good God has done for you? An answer to prayer, a job opportunity, healing in your body, or maybe a financial breakthrough?

_____

_____

_____

_____

Roadblocks----What roadblocks have presented themselves to you in a positive or negative way? How did you respond?

_____

_____

_____

_____

Exits----Did you see any you needed to take during your week? Like for example, did you feel God was bidding you to exit a hurtful relationship? Or, maybe God was asking you to take an exit from your current job.

_____

_____

_____

_____

Yield Signs----Were there any situations where you had the opportunity to take a purposeful pause before you reacted to someone or something?

_____

_____

_____

_____

Detours----Did you notice any detours God was trying to take you on? If so, what were they?

_____

_____

_____

_____

Shortcuts----Lastly, many times God will save us from repeating the same mistakes by taking us through a shortcut so we bypass the temptation. Did you recognize God moving like this in your life this week? If so, how?

_____

_____

_____

_____

Section Two: Practical Life Application

Fill in the blanks:

"Then the man said, 'Let me_____, for it is daybreak.' But Jacob replied, 'I will not let you go unless you_____ me.' The man asked him, 'What is your name?' 'Jacob,' he answered. Then the man said, 'Your name will no longer be Jacob, but _____, because you have struggled with God and with man and have overcome.'" Genesis 32:26-28

What does the name Jacob mean?

_____

_____

_____

What does the name Israel mean?

_____

_____

_____

What kind of a battle can you be in that God cannot prevail?

_____

_____

_____

_____

In the Bible, God changed people's names because the new name represented something important God was going to do in and through them. Dig deeper—read *Revelation 2:17*. Seek God as to what your new name might be and why.

Write your new name below.

_____

_____

_____

_____

Chapter Six

Pause and Consider This

"This is how the birth of Jesus Christ came about: His mother Mary was pledged to be married to Joseph, but before they came together, she was found to be with child through the Holy Spirit. Because Joseph her husband was a righteous man and did not want to expose her to public disgrace, he had in mind to divorce her quietly. But after he considered this, an angel of the Lord appeared to him in a dream and said, 'Joseph son of David, do not be afraid to take Mary home as your wife, because what is conceived in her is from the Holy Spirit. She will give birth to a son, and you are to give him the name Jesus, because he will save his people from their sins.' All this took place to fulfill what the Lord had said through the prophet: The virgin will be with child and will give birth to a son, and they will call him Immanuel which means, 'God with us.' When Joseph woke up, he did what the angel of the Lord commanded him and took Mary home as his wife. But he had no union with her until she gave birth to a son. And he gave him the name Jesus." Matthew 1:18-25

I heard a story not long ago about a man who had been married for ten years. They had a son. The relationship had some troubles, and the man found himself longing for something or someone else. He started having an affair with a woman at his office. This went on for some time. Then finally one night, he came home, sat down with his wife and told her he did not love her anymore. He had found someone else, and he wanted a divorce. She listened to how he had fallen out of love with her and how he did not mean to hurt her. Then she walked away; not a word spoken, she just got up and walked away. She went to the kitchen, pulled out a notebook, sat down at the table and began to write. Her husband came in the kitchen before bed and noticed she was writing. When he got up the next morning, she was still at the table writing. She asked him to sit down, and then she said, "I will grant you a divorce under a two conditions. Condition one—you wait to file for the divorce for thirty days. Condition two—I want you to carry me from our bedroom to the front door everyday just like you did when you carried me into our home on our wedding day." He stared at her and thought it was an odd request, but he agreed. Day one came. He scooped her up and carried her to the door noticing she had begun to look a little older. The next day came, and he carried her to the door. Day three came and went; then day four. After a few days of this, he started noticing her. He started noticing her perfume and the way she felt in his arms, how her hair flowed and complimented her face. Days went by and then weeks. He could feel himself feeling something for her again. He started looking forward to carrying her. Their little boy would make comments about how strong his daddy was for carrying his mom. He knew his love was back for her, so he went to the woman he was having an affair with and told her it was over because he was still in love with his wife. The next few days as he carried her, he noticed she was getting lighter. He didn't pay much attention, but he did notice. On the last day of their agreement, he stopped by the flower shop, picked her up some flowers and rushed home to announce his renewed love for her. He ran in the house and up the stairs where she was laying on the bed. He ran over to her, handed her the flowers and then asked for forgiveness... but she was gone. She had died. You see, she knew she was dying of cancer, and she knew she did not have long to live. She didn't want her son to have a memory of how his dad left his mom when she was dying, so to spare the relationship between a father and a son, she gave her husband a chance to pause and consider for a moment... to reconsider his decision to divorce. There is power in a pause. This woman was made for more and saved for something. She saved the son and father relationship and the husband's mind from guilt.

The story of Jesus does not start in Matthew but in Luke. Six months before the angel came to Mary, he went to Zechariah and Elizabeth. According to *Luke 1:56*, the angel Gabriel had just told Mary she was going to be pregnant by the Holy Spirit, and then she packed her bags and left to go stay at her cousin's house for three months. Listen, y'all, she traveled alone. Joseph did not come with her; he was not invited. In Matthew, it says Mary was found pregnant. "Found" means she was seen as being pregnant. In other words, she was showing. When Mary came home from visiting her cousin for three months, she was showing. Everyone could see she was pregnant. Can you imagine? Now everyone knew Mary had been up to something with somebody... but Joseph was not on the trip. To make matters worse, she was engaged to Joseph. Gifts had been exchanged, barters had been made. They were in their second stage of being engaged.

According to the law, Mary could have been stoned to death. All Mary knew was that she heard from the angel, went to visit her cousin, was now pregnant, and all she could do was trust God. She'd done the right thing. She had not sinned, but she couldn't really defend herself. Who would believe she was impregnated by the Holy Spirit? Have you ever found yourself in a similar position?

Mary's big problem was Joseph. I can imagine Joseph saying, "Okay, let me get this straight. You went to your cousin's a virgin, you hung out with your cousin for three months and then you came home pregnant. You're telling me the Holy Spirit impregnated you? Is this the yarn you're spinning, Mary?" After pondering these Scriptures, trying to put myself in either one of their positions, I had to ask... I know that Jesus needed to come through a virgin, but the Word does not say He needed to come through an *engaged* virgin. So why did Joseph need to be a part of this? Why did God pick a virgin who was engaged? Surely there were plenty of virgins who were not engaged at the time. The only logical explanation is there is something for us to glean from Joseph's response to all of this. I kept reading the Scriptures and rereading. I read that Joseph decided to put Mary away quietly because he did not want her to be hurt. *Matthew 1:19-20 says, "Because Joseph her husband was a righteous man and did not want to expose her to public disgrace, he had in mind to divorce her*

66

quietly. But after he considered this, an angel of the Lord appeared to him in a dream and said, 'Joseph, son of David, do not be afraid to take Mary home as your wife, because what is conceived in her is from the Holy Spirit.'"

But after Joseph **considered**, after he had taken a **pause,** the angel came to him in a dream. When Joseph woke up, *Matthew 1:24* says he married Mary. There was no planning of the wedding, no tux fittings or dress alterations, nor were there flowers ordered or a cake tasting, no fancy invitations or menu planning, or even a dress rehearsal. Nope, the Scripture says, he woke up and married her. Watch this y'all... when the baby was born, the Word of God told Joseph to name Him Jesus. This is so powerful, because in this divine moment, Joseph could have saved face. He could have gotten all the gossipers off his back if he would have named the baby Joseph, little Joe, Joe Joe... anything but Jesus. He could have redeemed his reputation, but because Joseph stopped to consider another way, because he took a powerful pause, Jesus was born. Wow! Could you imagine if we would stop when we are faced with such opposition and consider another alternative, take a powerful pause and consider allowing God to speak to us in the situation we are in? This is a life changer, my friend. We must train ourselves for battle. I think one of our training procedures should be taking a pause to consider what God wants to say on the matter, and what God wants to do or express in the moment.

I was attending an all-day conceal and carry class a few years back. The instructor shared a story about a police department who had purchased some new Taser guns. The rep who had sold the department the guns said the batteries should last nine months. He also instructed the police officers to test the Tasers before each shift for five minutes. At the end of forty-five days, the batteries were completely gone and to purchase new ones was around a hundred dollars for each battery. The chief of police called the rep who had sold the guns and explained the dilemma. He then told the chief to have the police officers test every Taser being used for five *seconds* before each shift. One day, a police officer was out doing a routine check when a suspect took off on foot. The police officer chased him down, caught up with him and tased him for five seconds. The suspect kept on running. Why? Because being tased for five seconds is not enough to stop someone. You see, you will never rise to the occasion beyond your training. You will only rise to the level of training when challenged with the occasion. He had trained himself to shoot the Taser for five seconds, so when it came time to tase someone, he only shot it for five seconds and released the trigger. His training had become his automatic response.

We must train ourselves to "pause and consider" in our decision making because we need to allow God the room and space to speak to us.

Jesus was always stopping and pausing to consider. When Jesus was about to feed the five thousand, He paused, held the bread up, thanked His Father for the provision, and then God multiplied it *(Matthew 14:19-20)*. When the Pharisees and Sadducees brought the woman who was caught in adultery to Jesus, Jesus paused, drew a line in the sand and began to write. I can't prove what He wrote, but could He have been writing the sins of the people standing there ready to stone her to death? Maybe He wrote the name of the man she was sleeping with in the sand. You notice the Pharisees didn't bring him to Jesus *(John 8:4)*.

What about when Jesus was told Lazarus was dying? He took a three day pause and considered before He went to Lazarus. I'm not sure you're aware of this but people were raised from the dead many times in the Bible, just never after three days. It was believed that the spirit hovered near the body for three days, but after the third day, it left. Jesus raised Lazarus from the dead after four days in the grave. This was truly a miracle that no one could ignore or deny. I could go on and on, but I'll end with this famous pause to consider... the pause of the grave. Jesus paused in His own resurrection. He paused, and then He rose above the grave, above death, above the nay-sayers, above the devil, above the lies, above doubt and unbelief. With a moment to pause and consider, you could change the trajectory of your life. You were made for more than an unconsidered pause and you were saved for something.

Don't miss what God has for you, because if you noticed, Joseph was going to do the right and noble thing. He was going to divorce Mary quietly. You might be thinking, *They were only engaged so why did he say he had to divorce her secretly?* In the Jewish tradition, there were three phases to marriage. The first phase was the barter phase where the groom would offer the family of the bride something of value for the daughter's hand in marriage. The second phase was the actual engagement. The final phase was consummating the marriage. Jewish tradition meant if you were in any of these phases of marriage, a divorce would be required to end it. Although Joseph was going to do right by Mary, he still needed to pause, because even if everything looks great on paper and sounds like the noble thing to do, it does not mean it's the will of God for your life. You were made for more and saved for something. Consider taking a pause next time you're faced with a decision in your life. Because Joseph paused and considered, he played a huge part in bringing Jesus into the world with the name, Jesus. You see, in the Jewish culture, the fathers always gave the babies their names. When I stopped and thought about it, I realized God knew the culture as well, and Jesus' Father gave Him *His* name, in keeping with the culture.

If you enjoyed this chapter, please subscribe to my YouTube channel where I create three to five minute Vertical Hope videos. Search Michele Davenport with one "L."

Section One: Awareness of God's Presence

Faith Builder----What is something good God has done for you? An answer to prayer, a job opportunity, healing in your body, or maybe a financial breakthrough?

Roadblocks----What roadblocks have presented themselves to you in a positive or negative way? How did you respond?

_____

_____

_____

_____

Exits----Did you see any you needed to take during your week? Like for example, did you feel God was bidding you to exit a hurtful relationship? Or, maybe God was asking you to take an exit from your current job.

_____

_____

_____

_____

Yield Signs----Were there any situations where you had the opportunity to take a purposeful pause before you reacted to someone or something?

_____

_____

_____

_____

Detours----Did you notice any detours God was trying to take you on? If so, what were they?

_____

_____

_____

_____

Shortcuts----Lastly, many times God will save us from repeating the same mistakes by taking us through a shortcut so we bypass the temptation. Did you recognize God moving like this in your life this week? If so, how?

_____

_____

_____

_____

Section Two: Practical Life Application

When was the last time you were faced with a decision and you sought God before you made a choice?

_____

_____

_____

_____

What was the outcome after seeking God through prayer first?

_____

_____

_____

_____

Be honest, what have you trained yourself to do when you're faced with a big decision? Do you call your mamma or a friend? Do you talk to you husband or wife first? Do you do research or seek council? Or, have you trained yourself to sit quietly and pray about the circumstance before any other option? Remember, we always ask the person we think has the answer first.

_____

_____

_____

_____

Have you ever been in a situation like Mary where all you could do was trust God to show people the truth because what it looked like wasn't what it truly was? How did you handle it?

_____

_____

_____

_____

Is there a situation in your life right now that you could consider a powerful pause before making a decision? If so, are you willing to wait on God before making a move? If you're doing the study in a group setting, then pause right here and ask others to pray with you about what's going on in your life.

_____

_____

_____

_____

Chapter Seven

Now I Know

"Now Elijah the Tishbite, from Tishbe in Gilead, said to Ahab, 'As the Lord, the God of Israel, lives, whom I serve, there will be neither dew nor rain in the next few years except at my word.' Then the word of the Lord came to Elijah, 'Leave here, turn eastward and hide in the Kerith Ravine, east of the Jordan. You will drink from the brook, and I have ordered the ravens to feed you there.' So he did what the Lord had told him. He went to the Kerith Ravine, east of the Jordan, and stayed there. The ravens brought him bread and meat in the morning and bread and meat in the evening, and he drank from the brook." 1 Kings 17:1-6

Did you notice Elijah didn't have any introduction? No childhood story leading up to his visitation. We didn't get a backdrop of his life on how God raised him up in the shadows of great leaders. How his mother was a noble woman, and his father was a man who feared God. How his brothers were all prophets and rulers. No, we weren't introduced to his parents or siblings, uncles or aunties. He just showed up and said, "As sure as the Lord lives, there will not be any rain for the next few years."

Day in and day out, twice a day, the ravens brought Elijah two meals, which was a miracle in itself. Ravens are considered scavenger birds; they will eat anything. It's shocking the ravens didn't eat Elijah's food. As Elijah sat beside the brook, called Kerith, which means "cut off and put away," he enjoyed the provisions of God. I can see him kicked back on a rock, propping his feet up on a tree stump, listening to the gentle wind blow as he basked in the sun, eating some of God's groceries. He was safe from all famine. In *1 Kings 17:7-9*, the Word of God says, *"Sometime later the brook dried up, because there had not been any rain in the land. Then the word of the Lord came to him: 'Go at once to Zarephath of Sidon and stay there. I have commanded a widow in that place to supply you with food.'"*

Fun fact—did you know the Bible says the word "go" 1187 times? In my life, when God tells me to go, it's always for the benefit of someone else. Don't get me wrong, I always get blessed through the act of obedience, but the reason I'm called to go is for someone else. When God first called me to go to Chiang Mai, Thailand, I said, "Yes, Lord." An announcement was placed in the church bulletin to anyone who would be interested in joining the team. From there a team emerged, and we traveled half way across the world to volunteer at Abba House, a ministry that rescues and ministers to children who have fallen prey to the sex trafficking industry. We all bonded in ways we will never forget as we worked for months on our curriculum, our plan of action when we arrived, where we would go in our spare time and who we could minister to while we were there. We dove deep into the Word of God and made plans to teach English and Bible stories to the children during the day. Then we would catch a songthaew to hold street ministry in the evenings at the third largest outside market in the world. I remember one night in particular. I was trying to witness to a young man working in one of the clothing shops, and it wasn't going well. I had a salvation tract in my hand, and I told this young man if he read it and prayed about what it said, I would come back the next night and pay more for the pants than he was asking. Typically, this is not how you barter at a market. You usually try to barter them down a bit, but for me, his salvation was hanging in the balance, so I went for it. He agreed. The next night, he gave his life to the Lord. You see when God says, "Go," He already has a plan for when you arrive, just like He had a plan when Elijah arrived at the gate where the widow woman was preparing herself and her son to die.

1 Kings 17:10-12 says, "So he went to Zarephath. When he came to the town gate, a widow was there gathering sticks. He called to her and asked, 'Would you bring me a little water in a jar so I may have a drink?' As she was going to get it, he called, 'And bring me, please, a piece of bread.' 'As surely as your Lord lives,' she replied, 'I don't have any bread, only a handful of flour in a jar and a little oil in a jug. I am gathering a few sticks to take home and make a meal for myself and my son, that we may eat it and die.'"

Wait a minute… it's one thing to ask for a drink, but to ask for all she had? Wow! That's gutsy. Listen, you don't want to miss this amazing teaching in between the verses and the Hebrew language. She was preparing her last meal before she and her son were going to die. It's interesting to note, the word "flour," in Hebrew, means "strip off" and "oil" means "fruitful." God was stripping off her hopelessness, so her life would once again be fruitful.

There were many widows in that day. You might be wondering, *How do you know, Michele?* I'm glad you asked. Jesus said in *Luke 4:25-26, "I assure you that there were many widows in Israel in Elijah's time, when the sky was shut up for three and a half years and there was a severe famine throughout the land. Yet Elijah was not sent to any of them, but to a widow in Zarephath in the Region of Sidon."* I believe while the widow woman gathered sticks, she prayed. The Bible does not mention that she did, but that's what I believe. In *1 Kings 17:13-14*, Elijah goes on to say, *"'don't be afraid, go home and do as you have said. BUT FIRST, make a small loaf of bread for me from what you have and bring it to me, and then make something for yourself and your son. For this is what the Lord, the God of Israel, says: 'The jar of flour will not be used up and the jug of oil will not run dry until the day the Lord sends rain on the land.'"*

In other words… BUT FIRST, before you give up, before you quit your life, before your hope dies, before you get the shovel out and start burying your marriage, your relationship, your job, your mortgage, and your right to live, do as I say… and see the hand of God move in your life. Obedience starts with belief. God can't multiply what we can't recognize. In verse fifteen, the Scripture says she went and did what Elijah said and there was enough food every day for the woman, her family and Elijah. *"For the jar of flour was not used up and the jug of oil did not run dry, in keeping with the word the Lord had spoken by Elijah" (1 Kings 17:16)*. We serve a more than enough God, but we act like we serve a God of lack, a God who might show up or might not, a God who sometimes cares and sometimes doesn't. Listen y'all, her last meal became the entry point for many more. Some of you are looking for your provision in the obvious place when it's in the most un-obvious place. God sent Elijah to a widow. He was a foreigner in Jezebel's home town, a pagan nation that was required by law to take care of their prophets, but instead, God had unclean scavenger birds feed him and a widow offer him lodging and food. What a faith builder being built by the very hand of God in Elijah's life and the widow's life, but also something else deserves a mention—what about the faith of her son whom she was preparing to die with her? He was a witness to all the miracles as well.

Don't you know, y'all, every time the woman dipped her hand into the flour and poured out the oil, it was a faith builder for anyone who witnessed this miracle? I can just see it in my mind's eye, how that might have looked. She woke up early in the morning to prepare for the day. First thing on the list after her morning routine was time to prepare the bread. As she walked over to the flour, it was still the same amount she had on the day she met Elijah—just enough for a loaf. But it was different because it was just enough for a loaf *every* day. It wasn't any more than when she was preparing to die; it was the same. But now God was in it. God had made a promise because the widow chose to believe that the flour would be there tomorrow. As she poured the flour out onto the bread table, and as the last bit of flour hit the surface, she stood the jar up... and there it was, folks, enough flour left for tomorrow still sitting and settling into the bottom of the jar. She reached for the jug of oil and repeated the process of faith. To me, it's one of the most beautiful pictures of faith, but as we read on to *1 Kings 17:17-18*, it also becomes one of the saddest acts of unbelief.

1 Kings 17:17-18, "Some time later the son of the woman who owned the house became ill. He grew worse and worse, and finally stopped breathing. She said to Elijah, 'What do you have against me, man of God? Did you come to remind me of my sin and kill my son?'"

God performed a miracle when He saved the widow and her son from death. He could have used any widow that day to feed Elijah, but God sent Elijah to her. Just a few sentences later though, her son died. Be careful that we don't forget about the miracles God has already done in our lives. The Lord brought the Israelites out of Egypt miraculously, but as soon as they got out of Egypt, they started doubting God's ability to sustain them. Don't you forget the God who brought you out of sickness, who brought you out of debt, out of an abusive relationship, out of alcoholism, divorce and a hopeless situation. Many times, we disconnect from the God who created the entire universe and the God who created us. He is the same in one. Nothing is too big for our God. Listen to what I hear the widow woman say, "I don't want to have anything to do with you, Mr. Prophet Man. All you came here to do is remind me of my sin and kill my son." Now this is a great time to remember the Word of God, which He spoke to her through Elijah. He told her that her jug of oil and jar of flour would not run out until rain moistened the earth again. Remember, they were still in the three and half year drought, which Elijah prophesied would happen. What we know for sure up to this point is God sent Elijah to a widow woman, this particular widow woman, to save her and her son through a miracle. We know the jug of oil had not run out, neither had the jar of flour.

As I was sitting at my kitchen table when we were stationed in Knoxville, Tennessee, God began to speak to me. He told me I would be traveling, ministering to the brokenhearted, bringing freedom to the captives, nationally and internationally. As I sat there in awe of God and His incredible plan for my life, I said, "God I want to believe you, but help my unbelief. Send me someone to confirm this word, someone who would not know what You have spoken to my heart." I was walking down the hall at Knoxville Christian Center, my church at the time, getting prepared to teach. As I was headed down the hall, a woman passed by me. She grabbed my arm and turned me around. She said, "Thus saith the Lord, 'You will be traveling, speaking life changing messages to the brokenhearted, and your words will set the captives free. You will travel nationally and internationally.'" Oh my, y'all! I fell to the ground crying and sobbing at her feet as she stood there. She said, "I was not supposed to be here right now, but I got locked out of the church and had to wait for someone to let me in." Wow! God's timing is perfect. Immediately after she confirmed God's Word, I wanted to say, "Get the worship team together, grab some clothes and a travel bag, prepare a team and let's start loading the bus." Little did I know that just because I asked God to confirm His Word, did not mean the Word was going to come to pass right in that moment. I had no idea I was going to sit in God's waiting room for years as He prepared my character for the call.

During the next fourteen years, I cleared my desk off more times than I can remember, but I kept moving forward. I've seen and heard of many people who get a Word from the Lord, and they literally sit and wait in a corner for it to come to pass. Not me. I taught classes, got involved in prison ministry, wrote four books, homeschooled my girls and received my Associates in Biblical Studies. I said all that, not to puff myself up, but to tell you part of God preparing me for the call was training me for the call. Each class I led taught me how to communicate the Word of God in my own personal way while learning how to speak in front of people. Prison ministry taught me how to handle an array of different personalities while giving me a deeper heart for the abandoned and brokenhearted. Each book I wrote taught me humility because English was my worst subject by far. Homeschooling taught me patience, organizational skills and about staying committed until the end. You see, the very tears I cried, the desk I cleared, the frustration I felt was just as much a part of God's plan for my life as setting captives free. I had to be in God's waiting room because that's where He grew me into becoming the woman of God He had called me to become. If there are no challenges, there is no change!

One Thursday morning while running on my treadmill, I was crying out to God, because that's what I did about every three months when it seemed like God had forgotten the clear blue morning at my Knoxville, Tennessee kitchen table. The faster I ran, the more I screamed out to God, "Don't You know how old I am? I've been faithful, God, where are You? I'm about to give up, I'm about to let go of the hope rope, Lord. Please send someone a Word for me, either in a dream, a vision, or in Your Word. I need to know I'm still on the right track."

I was hopeless and I needed a flour and oil experience in my life. I needed a pouring out experience. I needed to know the drought was almost over.

That Saturday morning my friend Tammi Crowley contacted me through Facebook. She said, "Michele, I had a dream about you." She explained what she saw. As she watched in her dream, she could see me fulfilling my purpose, and it was far better than I could have imagined or prayed for. "Jesus was laughing and full of joy," she said, "Michele it's just around the corner." She encouraged my heart that day, and my soul was refreshed. This was on a Saturday morning when she reached out to me. I asked Tammi, "When did God give you this dream?" She said, "Thursday night."

Oh my gosh, y'all! It was Thursday morning when I was crying out to God. As if this was not enough, she went on to tell me it was even a miracle that she was able to reach out to me on Facebook because she was not supposed to be able to get internet. Come on, don't tell me we don't serve a personal God! Over the years, God has sent me my share of Elijahs to encourage me not to give up, give out, or give into the impossible, because He is a God of the impossible.

Fourteen years ago, a lady whom I respect highly, prophesied over me. She said, "Faith Builders ministry would take off when a lady came along side of me in resources and prayer." I've met many women along my way, and I would think, *Are you the one? Nope, okay. Are you the one? No, you're not. How about you? No, okay. You must be the one. Yes, you're the one.* Then she would serve and be called to leave. I would say, "Hey where are you going? I think you're the one." Ha ha ha!

In 2016, I finally met the one, at least one of the ones, through a miracle meeting of the souls. You see, when I start missing my mom,

I usually do something we did together. We used to go antiquing together. I was having one of those missing my mamma kind of days, so I went into a place I was told about called Stacks Depot. I walked in and fell in love with a dining room light, so I asked about it. A woman named Pam began to explain to me that she had made it. She knew a lot about antiques. She had been in the business for years, and she was also the owner of Stacks Depot. She took me to the back of the shop, kind of like a warehouse. I began to share with her, and she with me. In this moment, we became friends in the Spirit. I bought the light. She told me she would tell my Superman how to hang it. We got the light home and hanging it was not as simple as we had originally thought. Marty, a.k.a. Superman, blew out half our electricity. I called Pam, and she said she would make a call. A few minutes later, we were talking to someone named Matthew. He said he would be right over to hang our light and fix the problem at no charge on a Saturday.

As he was hanging our light, we started talking about Jesus. He asked what church we attended. We told him, but we also mentioned we were looking for a church closer to where we lived. We informed him we had tried all the churches around us. He asked, "Have you been to Belton Assembly?" We said, "No." He went on to tell us that we would love it, and we should consider trying his church. Superman and I both agreed to go the next morning. Minutes after being in the service, Marty looked at me and said, "We are home." My new friend, Pam, went to the same church; we have been friends ever since.

Faith Builders did take off, and Pam was one of the ones. She did have incredible resources, and she is a praying woman. In 2015, Faith Builders ministries partnered with Belton Assembly of God, meaning they believed in Faith Builders' vision a hundred percent— me ministering to the hurting women and Marty to hurting men. You see, what I learned is the church was part of the one, and many people along my journey were parts of the one, because each one sowed a measure in me when I was sitting beside a brook waiting for the ravens to feed me, taking a powerful pause as God developed me into becoming the woman He created me to be. Each person, over the years, had something in them that made them the one in that moment of my life. All of the ones who showed up in my life for a season helped me realize I was made for more and saved for something.

In 2015, Marty started a men's group through Belton Assembly, and our church also provided the venue and supported two women's conferences and six Friday night women's church services for Faith Builders as well. It was an incredible year. What's ironic is I had prayed the Jabez prayer many times, "Lord, expand my territory." I thought to expand my territory could only happen in a mega church, but God moved us to a smaller church to expand our territory. You see, this is how our human minds work, we think bigger equals better. God did the not-so-obvious, not the obvious. Never let your circumstances control what you know by the Spirit.

The widow woman's son did die. She wanted to walk away from God and Elijah. Watch this… she was going to give up on God while she was still in the middle of her last miracle. The oil was still pouring and the flour was still in the jar. In the middle of a miracle, she was faced with another opportunity to believe that the same God who gave her and her son back life once before, could do it again. Oh my, this should speak to someone reading today! Right now, many of you are living in a miracle God has provided, but something else has come your way, and you say, "I can't believe for this." Come on, all of us have had some kind of faith builder in our lives to stand on when we are faced with a challenge, whether it's one you're going through now or one you have already gone through.

In 1 Kings 17:19-24, Elijah says, 'Give me your son.' He took him from her arms carried him to the upper room where he was staying, and laid him on his bed. Then he cried out to the Lord, 'O Lord my God, have you brought tragedy also upon this widow I am staying with, by causing her son to die?' Then he stretched himself out on the boy three times and cried to the Lord, 'O Lord, my God, let this boy's life return to him.' The Lord heard Elijah's cry, and the boy's life returned to him, and he lived. Elijah picked up the boy and carried him down from the room into the house. He gave him to his mother and said, 'Look your son is alive!' Then the woman said to Elijah,

'Now I know that you are a man of God and that the word of the Lord from your mouth is truth.'''

This is such an exciting piece of Scripture... between a prayer and a stretch, the boy came back to life. Stretch those prayers, y'all! Lay it all down and believe the promises God has given you. I did notice the Word said Elijah went upstairs by himself with the boy. God performed a miracle the mother could not be a part of. Have you ever had need of a miracle you couldn't believe for? Listen, the widow woman had a man in her inner circle that could act on her behalf. Elijah was the deliverer of the miracle. Right now, you're one of three: the widow woman in need of a miracle, an Elijah—the answer to someone else's prayer for a miracle, or if you have the faith, you can be both—in need of a miracle and also willing to be an answer to someone else's prayer.

I about fell out of my chair as I read *verse 24, "Then the woman said to Elijah, "Now I know that you are a man of God and that the word of the Lord from your mouth is truth."*

What!?! No, she didn't just say, "**Now I know.**" You mean she didn't know Elijah spoke truth when she used her last bit of oil and flour to make Elijah something to eat? He said if she gave him what little she had that day, her jug of oil and jar of flour would not run out until God sent rain. Rain still had not come. She still had plenty of flour and oil. She was still right in middle of her miracle. Before we start judging her too harshly, let's direct it back to you and me. *What do you mean, Michele, "Now I know"?* After God has seen you through your desert moments, death, sickness, loss of beyond comprehensible measure, are you still thinking, *What do you mean, "Now I know,"* *Michele?* Even though God has done a great miracle yesterday, you forget you're still in the miracle today. Sometimes we just need to allow God the flour and oil moments in our lives, the stripping off so we can live our lives in fruitfulness. Because we were made for more and saved for something. Elijah was made for more than being a prophet; that's what he did, but it wasn't the sum of who he was. He was also made to bring life to a widow and her son!

If you enjoyed this chapter, please subscribe to my YouTube channel where I create three to five minute Vertical Hope videos. Search Michele Davenport with one "L."

Section One: Awareness of God's Presence

Faith Builder----What is something good God has done for you? An answer to prayer, a job opportunity, healing in your body, or maybe a financial breakthrough?

_____

_____

_____

_____

Roadblocks----What roadblocks have presented themselves to you in a positive or negative way? How did you respond?

_____

_____

_____

_____

Exits----Did you see any you needed to take during your week? Like for example, did you feel God was bidding you to exit a hurtful relationship? Or, maybe God was asking you to take an exit from your current job.

_____

_____

_____

_____

Yield Signs----Were there any situations where you had the opportunity to take a purposeful pause before you reacted to someone or something?

_____

_____

_____

_____

Detours----Did you notice any detours God was trying to take you on? If so, what were they?

_____

_____

_____

_____

Shortcuts----Lastly, many times God will save us from repeating the same mistakes by taking us through a shortcut so we bypass the temptation. Did you recognize God moving like this in your life this week? If so, how?

_____

_____

_____

_____

Section Two: Practical Life Application

Has God ever called you to go somewhere, or to somebody, and you didn't understand why until you were obedient?

_____

_____

_____

_____

When was the last time you experienced a flour and oil miracle in your life? If you never have, then may I say, you are believing and living too small.

_____

_____

_____

_____

At this point and time in your life, who would you consider yourself to be: an Elijah—being the miracle and the answer to someone else's prayer, the widow—the one in need of the miracle, or both—the one in need of a miracle but also willing to be the miracle in someone else's life?

_____

_____

_____

_____

When was your "Now I know You are God and Your Word is truth"
moment? I experienced my moment with God in that way, sitting
alone in my base housing in Belton, Missouri.

_____

_____

_____

_____

Challenge:

Next time you believe you hear God tell you to become an answer
to someone else's prayer, act on it, then record the results. I'm at the
point in my life where I try to look for ways I can be an answer to
someone else's prayer.

Try it, the results are crazy good!

_____

_____

_____

_____

Chapter Eight

Cold Case Christian

"My food is to do the will of Him who sent me and finish the work." John 4:34

Webster's Dictionary defines "cold case" as "an unsolved criminal investigation that has stopped being actively pursued because of a lack of evidence." These cases are still considered open, but they remain inactive unless new evidence is uncovered. Reasons for these unsolved cases could include an unknown identity of either the victim or the perpetrator or even an unknown, but suspicious, cause of death. There is a parallel to this concept in the spiritual realm as well. Some of us are walking around "spiritually dead" from an unknown cause. Maybe we started out alive and well in the body of Christ, but something along the way came and choked the life out of us... and we became "Cold Case Christians." These cases are unsolved because the cause of "spiritual death" is yet unknown. However, cracking these cases is a must if we are to return to "being alive in Christ."

Several years back, I wrote a weekly column for the newspaper called *Choices are for the Living*, which eventually turned into my fourth book. I remember God speaking loudly in my spirit one day about a rapidly growing spiritual eating disorder in the body of Christ. This disorder was leading the believers to a spiritual morgue with toe tags labeled, "Bulimic Jane Doe," "Obese Jane Doe," and "Anorexic Jane Doe."

Here is where our "Cold Case Christian" files become hot again. I believe the Spirit has given us the new evidence needed to finally solve these puzzling cases. He's equipped us with the tools we need to identify both the victims and the causes of "spiritual death." And He's even pointed us in the right direction using Biblical examples. In light of this new evidence, I want to spend the next three chapters investigating a few "Cold Case Christians" we find in Scripture. First up for our investigation is Peter.

Before we begin the journey of inspecting the evidence of the crime scenes, please allow me to get into character by putting on my trench coat and glasses, and grabbing my notebook and pen. Let me dust off the boxes, get my gloves ready for inspection, and prepare for a long trial.

First Case: Peter

Crime Scene: The Book of John

Cause of Death: Spiritual Bulimia

Evidence: A boat, a net, and a folded napkin

Definition of "Spiritual Bulimia": condition found in people who eat and eat the Word of God until it doesn't make sense, or it becomes too hard to believe. It can't possibly be real, so they purge it out.

When Whitney, my oldest daughter, wouldn't eat well, we used to do a circus act, complete with tightrope walking, juggling and flame throwing, to get her to take just one bite. She really only liked mashed potatoes. So what would any awesome parent do? We fed her mashed potatoes every day, until one day she started gagging when we tried to feed her. We couldn't say mashed potatoes without her gagging. We couldn't eat them around her, beside her or behind her back. We couldn't even say, "Please pass the mashed potatoes." Sometimes that's how we act when God tries to feed us the truth of His Word, we start gagging. *You want me to forgive_____? Gag! You want me to give_____ money? Gag! You want me to teach a*

Bible class? Gag, Gag, Gag. *You want me to quit my job and apply for another one?* Gag! *You want me to be the bigger person and ask for forgiveness for the part I played in the argument?* Gag, Gag, Gag, and just for emphasis, Gag! See, many of us are not much different than my little baby who used to gag at eating mashed potatoes.

I'm highly allergic to buckwheat. One time, I was staying at a friend's house while speaking at a women's weekend conference. Her husband had made breakfast for us and it was time to dig in. As I started eating, I took a bite of toast, and immediately, the Holy Spirit said, "Spit it out. It has buckwheat in it." I spit it out and then asked John if the toast had buckwheat in it. He grabbed the loaf of bread, read the label and said, "Yes, it does." Listen, we need to train ourselves to not only listen to the Holy Spirit, but to obey, to eat the Words of the Spirit. Listening and obeying saved me from a trip to the emergency room, or possibly even death, because at that time, I was not carrying an EpiPen.

Another reason we purge out the Word of God is we don't like what it says, and our situation looks hopeless. Sometimes, y'all, we purge out the truth to swallow a lie. *Romans 1:25, "They exchanged the truth for a lie, and worshipped and served created things rather than the Creator, who is forever praised."* This is one of the saddest Scriptures in the Bible to me. Remember Eve in the garden? She purged out the truth of God for a lie from the enemy. God said, "Don't eat from this one tree," Satan said, "Did God really say?"

Now… back to our first Biblical example of a "Cold Case Christian." We know who our spiritual toe tag belongs to—Peter, and where the crime scene is—the book of John. Let's start our investigation with some evidence—the folded napkin.

In *John 20*, we read about the empty tomb. Mary Magdalene went to Jesus' tomb and found the stone had been rolled away. She ran back to Peter and John and informed them someone had moved Jesus' body because the tomb was empty. John took off running way ahead of Peter. When John arrived at the tomb, he just peeked in, but he didn't go in. Peter, however, flew by John, went into the tomb and saw the strips of linen lying there where Jesus' feet would have been, as well as the burial napkin which would have been around Jesus' face. The cloth was folded up and placed at the head.

Let's investigate some, shall we? First of all, Jesus knew John would not enter the tomb, even if he did beat Peter there. But Jesus knew Peter would. Jesus had His attention and mind set on Peter all through *John 20-21*. I'll prove it since that is the responsibility of the investigator in a cold case. The word "saw," in Greek, means "to investigate." So when *John 20:6-7* said Peter saw the napkin and linens, what it's really saying is Peter investigated the scene. Peter did not just walk in the tomb and look around, but instead, he walked in and investigated the tomb. He looked under things, and maybe he picked up the linens, maybe he smelled them and checked for blood or rips in the fabric. He noticed the folded linen napkin at the head of the tomb.

I need to interject some facts right here. You need to know that all Jewish boys knew exactly what a folded napkin represented. They were all raised with this common knowledge. The folded napkin represented the master and the servant. The servant prepared the table, made the food, set the table, made sure drinks were in their containers, and then hid and watched the master, waiting for his cue to refill drinks or clear the table. If the master got up and wiped his beard, face and hands, then threw the napkin on the table, it meant he was done, clear the table. But, if the master wiped his face, beard and hands, and folded the napkin, placing it beside his plate, it meant he would be back, he wasn't done yet, it wasn't over. In other words, Jesus rose from the tomb and took time to fold His napkin and place it at the head. He was saying, y'all, it's not over, I'm not done yet, I'll be back! Oh my gosh, it's not over! He is not done! He is coming back! If you didn't get up and shout in this moment, you missed a great opportunity to show some love! I about fell out of my chair as I was typing this trying to remain as calm as possible until I finished the sentence. This is really good news!

Even after Jesus left a piece of evidence behind just for Peter, Peter walked out of the tomb and said, "I don't know what's going on here."

Listen, don't judge, even after Jesus has left plenty of evidence that He is real and active in your life, if you're honest, at times, you may also have said, "I don't know what's going on here. I don't know what to do, who to trust or what to think." Yes, you do! Believe the Word of God and keep walking, my friend. Train yourself to look for the evidence Jesus has left behind for you. Become a CIA in your own life—Christian in Action.

Three years ago, I went to have my routine mammogram. I left the office full of confidence. The yearly exam was done, and I was moving on to the next thing in my life. A few hours after I left the office, I received a phone call. They had found a mass on my left breast. They requested I come back the very next morning. I returned after standing on the Word of God. The doctor called me backed, showed me the mass and said she would retake the photo and then have a plan of action. She retook the x-ray and **NOTHING!** Nothing was there. What once was, was not anymore. Praise be to God! My Superman and I investigated the Word and stood on the Scriptures God gave us… and the outcome was astonishing. The x-ray technician even gave me the x-rays as proof. I have shared them many times at the conferences I have spoken at. My evidence was *Isaiah 53:5, "…by his stripes I am healed."* I know women die of breast cancer every day, and for this, I'm truly sorry and devastated over how much this disease has inflicted pain and loss upon the women of this world. I'm just sharing how we reacted and what we did when we were faced with the news.

The second piece of evidence used to convict Peter of becoming a "Cold Case Christian" is still found in John. In *John 20:11-18*, Jesus appeared to Mary Magdalene as she was crying. He said, "Don't cry. I'm returning to my Father, but I will be back, I'm not finished yet, it's not over, Mary. Now go tell the others." Mary ran back and told the others, including Peter. They did nothing. So let me see if we've got this right so far. Jesus said, on at least 24 occasions, that He would be crucified and raised up from the dead after three days. Jesus left evidence that He had risen by leaving the folded napkin in the tomb, which He knew Peter would investigate. Then He appeared to Mary and told her to go tell the others, but they did nothing.

Let's move onto the third piece of evidence revealing that Peter is slowly dying of spiritual bulimia, purging out what Jesus had told him before the crucifixion. We find in *John 20:19-20,* that Jesus had appeared to the disciples in the upper room behind closed doors. *Jesus said, 'Peace be with you,' then he showed them his wounds."* Have you ever asked yourself why Jesus showed them His wounds? It was as if He was saying to all of them, and us, "Look, you see I have wounds. I did not have to come up out of the grave with these wounds, but I did to show you I rose above My wounds and so can you." As Jesus stood in the upper room, He said this, *"Peace be with you, as the Father has sent Me I am sending you."* This is key, don't miss it. Jesus was showing us He rose above the pain of the past, above the wounds of the present, above the humiliation, above the enemies, above His current situation, because His eyes were on the things above. Jesus was showing Peter the evidence of the miracle. Jesus said, *"As the Father has sent Me, I am sending you."* Come on, y'all, we have been sent. Why are we not going?

We are retired from a twenty-five-year military career and everywhere we were sent, we were short-toured, meaning we never stayed very long. We stayed there until we were an answer to someone else's prayer, such as our neighbor getting saved, whoever that neighbor might be at the time. Then we immediately received orders to go. God made it abundantly clear that He was giving us our orders, and He was telling us to go.

The fourth piece of evidence is found in *John 20:24.* Jesus appeared again to the disciples in the upper room, but this time, He made a special visitation to Thomas, also known as Doubting Thomas. Jesus allowed Thomas to touch His wounds so he would believe. This happened in front of Peter, but it still does not appear that anything up to this point had Peter behaving like Jesus had truly risen just like He said He would. If you're keeping count, this is the third time Jesus had appeared after His resurrection. Here is where the story gets sad. In the upcoming moments, Peter takes on a fully embodied "bulimic Cold Case Christian" mentality, dying a spiritual death.

The last piece of evidence is a net, not just a net, but an empty net. *John 21:1-3, "Afterward Jesus appeared again to his disciples, by the Sea of Tiberius. It happened this way, Simon Peter, Thomas, Nathanael, from Cana in Galilee, the sons of Zebedee, and two other disciples were together. 'I'm going out to fish,' Simon Peter told them, and they said, 'We'll go with you.' So they went out and got into the boat, but that night they caught nothing."*

Not just one person followed Peter out of the will of God, not two, but six people followed Peter. The Greek word for "fish" here refers to the habit, not the occupation. Peter had walked with Jesus for over 3 years, and Jesus had mentioned on 24 different occasions that He would be crucified but raised from the dead. Jesus left evidence in the tomb—the folded napkin, and He even proved His power by raising Lazarus from the dead after four days of being in the tomb, which had never been done before. He had definitely proven He was well able to raise someone from the grave. But there is absolutely no evidence in the Bible that any of His disciples or followers believed He would actually rise again, including Peter. No one believed He had the power to raise Himself from the dead... except His enemies who crucified him. Listen, none of your friends may believe what God is calling you to do, but trust me, the enemy does.

The day after Jesus' death, the chief priests and the Pharisees went to Pilate and told him that when Jesus was still alive, He said after three days, He would rise again. Then Pilate told them to make the tomb as secure as possible. He put guards outside of the tomb and sealed a large stone in front of the tomb's entrance. They believed Jesus more than Peter or His followers did. Satan believes what God can do with your life more than you do. Jesus found Peter in a boat on the Sea of Galilee, back at his old habit, even after Jesus appeared to him on three different occasions so Peter would believe He had risen. This was all in addition to the evidence He left behind in the tomb for Peter.

This is where we find Peter purging out the truth for a lie—the lie that he could go back to his old habit and live happily ever after. In *John 21*, the disciples indeed went out to fish, but they fished all night and caught nothing. Jesus stood on the bank of Galilee, called out to them and told them to cast their nets on the right side. They obeyed and caught 153 fish. Even the number of fish they caught was a sign. In the Hebrew language, the letters are assigned a number along with a picture. The number one means "unity," the number five means "grace" and the number three means "completeness." Unity in Jesus brings grace and completeness. Jesus had a purpose for Peter's life beyond the shores of Galilee. Watch how Jesus wooed Peter back into the purpose for his life, because he, too, was made for more and saved for something.

Jesus asked Peter three times in *John 21:15-17, "Do you love me Peter?"* and goes on to say, *"Then feed My sheep."* Jesus told Peter in *Matthew 4:19, "Come follow me... and I will make you fishers of men."* In other words, Jesus was saying to Peter, "You once cast a net for a harvest of fish, but now you will cast into the deep for men and drag up a harvest of souls." Jesus also told Peter in the book of Matthew He would build His church upon the rock, which the word "rock" in Greek is "Petra," or Peter. *"Again Jesus said, Peace be with you as the Father has sent me, I am sending you" (John 20:21).* Peter's whole purpose was to go, go feed the sheep and to finish the work.

John 4:34, "My food is to do the will of him who sent me, and to finish the work."

Ephesians 2:10, "For we are God's workmanship, created in Christ Jesus to do good works, which God prepared in advance for us to do."

Peter was spiritually dying because he had allowed himself to become a "cold case bulimic believer," purging out the truth for a lie. Jesus said 24 times, "I will die, but I will be back on the third day." Are you becoming a "spiritually bulimic Christian" ready for the spiritual morgue? Has Jesus told you some things He's going to do, but you just don't believe it? He has given you all the signs—the folded napkin, the visitations, and the words of instruction. Don't go back to the old habits. You were made for more and saved for something. 1187 times in the Bible, it tells us to go. The great commission says, "GO!" I don't know what that looks like for you, but I think you do.

I know some of you reading this book are in the middle of your mess. You're hurting, desperate, down and out and disappointed over how things have turned out in your life, but can I tell you God's not finished, it's not over, He's not done, He will be back! Peter was a fisherman when Jesus met him, but don't miss this, he was made for more and saved for something. Jesus stood on the shore of Galilee and beckoned Peter back to Him. He asked him three times, "Peter do you love Me?" Peter kept saying, "Yes Lord, You know I do." Then Jesus finally said, on that confession, "Go feed My sheep." I believe with my whole heart chapters 20-21 of John were written in order to summon Peter back to his calling, because he was made for more than being a fisherman and saved for something bigger than fish. He went on to do great and mighty things for the kingdom of God before he was crucified upside down for his faith in Jesus, the One who took the time to redirect him. What are you doing with the information that Jesus died and was resurrected for you? You were made for more and saved for something, and I promise it is for more than just going to work and clocking in, for more than being a wife or a husband, a father or a mother. Even though these are very important aspects of your life, they are not all you were created for.

If you enjoyed this chapter, please subscribe to my YouTube channel where I create three to five minute Vertical Hope videos. Search Michele Davenport with one "L."

Section One: Awareness of God's Presence

Faith Builder----What is something good God has done for you? An answer to prayer, a job opportunity, healing in your body, or maybe a financial breakthrough?

_____

_____

_____

Roadblocks----What roadblocks have presented themselves to you in a positive or negative way? How did you respond?

_____

_____

_____

_____

Exits----Did you see any you needed to take during your week? Like for example, did you feel God was bidding you to exit a hurtful relationship? Or, was He asking you to take an exit from your current job?

_____

_____

_____

_____

Yield Signs----Were there any situations where you had the opportunity to take a purposeful pause before you reacted to someone or something?

_____

_____

_____

_____

Detours----Did you notice any detours God was trying to take you on? If so, what were they?

_____

_____

_____

_____

Shortcuts----Lastly, many times God will save us from repeating the same mistakes by taking us through a shortcut so we bypass the temptation. Did you recognize God moving like this in your life this week? If so, how?

_____

_____

_____

_____

Section Two: Practical Life Application:

Fill in the blanks:

"My_____ is to do the will of him who sent me, and to

_____ the work." John 4:34

"For we are God's _____, created in Christ Jesus to do good _____, which God prepared in _____ for us to do." Ephesians 2:10

If someone was investigating your life, would they find that you are a "bulimic Christian," meaning after God has shared something from His Word, do you believe it or purge it out because it seems unbelievable? Share your thoughts.

_____

_____

_____

_____

What's the last thing God told you He was going to do in your life? Has He done it yet? If not, what are you doing to keep the faith? What Scriptures are you standing on?

_____

_____

_____

_____

Have you ever purged out the truth of God for a lie of the enemy? Please write an example.

_____

_____

_____

What is your occupation? Homemaker, engineer, nurse, doctor, sales, dentist, waitress, store manager, painter, artist, writer, teacher, pastor, evangelist, mechanic, CNA, receptionist, etc.? Do you believe you were made for more and saved for something? If yes, what does that look like to you?

_____

_____

_____

_____

Has God placed a desire in your heart? If so, are you fulfilling the desire? If not, why?

_____

_____

_____

_____

Chapter Nine

Spiritual Obesity

*"The word of the Lord came to Jonah, go to the great city
of Nineveh and preach against it, because its wickedness
has come up before me." Jonah 1:1-2*

Has God ever called you to do something so intensely out of your comfort zone, that instead of entertaining His request for even one minute, you took off running? Has He ever caused you to trip over your own feet, to slow you down enough to hear and obey? Jonah is that guy. He is a runner. And he is another one of our Biblical "Cold Case Christians," because until now, the cause of his "spiritual death" was unknown. Let's get out this "cold case" and investigate why he is lying in a spiritual morgue with a toe tag labeled "Obesity."

Second Case: Jonah

Crime Scene: The book of Jonah

Cause of Death: Spiritual Obesity

Evidence: Running shoes, a ticket to Tarshish, and a map

Definition of "Spiritual Obesity": condition found in believers who are always "eating" the Word but never exercising their authority in Christ; they never use their gifts or talents. They are masters of hoarding the Word of God; listeners but not doers.

"The word of the Lord came to Jonah, go to the great city of Nineveh and preach against it, because its wickedness has come up before me." Jonah 1:1-2

Y'all need to know who Jonah was going to be facing in Nineveh because I'm not sure you or I would have obeyed either. Jonah would be facing 120,000 enemies of the Jews. To walk across the city of Nineveh would take three days, and he needed to walk across it announcing the Word of the Lord. Jonah was not going to be standing on a mountaintop, prophesying over 200 people as they sat by a campfire singing *Kumbaya*. He was going to Nineveh, and they were in huge sin. They were skinning people alive and hanging their skin on the city walls, burning children, and sexual sin had grown rampant. These were some wicked people who did not want to be corrected or ministered to in any way.

Simply put, Jonah was a prophet who did not want to prophesy. He wanted 120,000 people to die. Jonah knew the Word of the Lord. He was full of God, but he grabbed his running shoes and ran. The evidence I want to examine at this time is the map. We already know he had running shoes, and he would hand a ticket over to board a boat headed to Tarshish. When we glance at the map, the distance from Gath-hepher, Jonah's hometown, to Tarshish, where Jonah was headed when the storm came, would have been 2500 miles. It was only 500 miles to Nineveh, but 2500 miles to Tarshish. It's like Jonah said, "I would rather be 2500 miles out of the will of God than 500 miles in it." I've been there... have you?

As I was studying the Scriptures in the book of Jonah, I realized some of the best news in the whole book was found in Jonah 1:4, *"The Lord hurled a great storm at the boat."* Sometimes it's the storms in our lives that make us turn around. I travel to the prisons to minister to hurting women, and one comment I say to them often is, "Don't despise the whale because the whale is your jail. Had God not allowed you to be put in jail, you would have died on the streets between the needle and the bottle." Let me expound on this thought. You see, God provided the storm you're going through. It's His provision and intervention. Without the storm, the sailors would not have thrown Jonah overboard, and the whale wouldn't have swallowed him. Okay, the Bible does not say whale; it says a big fish. If Jonah had not been swallowed by a big fish, he would have drowned. You may be thinking, *If God did not send the storm, he would not have been thrown overboard, and he would not have needed a big fish to save him.* Yes, you're correct in your thinking, but God loved Jonah too much to leave him where he was, which was in complete disobedience. He loves you just as much… enough not to leave you in your disobedience. When you're running from God and He provides a storm, sometimes you need to look at that storm and not rebuke Satan, but thank God instead, because it's God's goodness and mercy to woo you back into His presence. Otherwise, you would keep running. Stop here and catch your breath, either from reading this paragraph or from running from God! Go ahead, I'll wait… I need to grab a snack anyway. I'm back. Are you breathing slower now, have you stopped running yet?

Storms show us where our faith is, sort of like our spiritual compass. Remember in *Mark 4:35, "Jesus said, 'Let's get in the boat and go to the other side.'"* A huge storm came upon them and the disciples began to freak out. They even accused Jesus of not caring that they were going to die. Jesus said in *Mark 4:40, "'Why are you so afraid, do you still have no faith?'"* I noticed Jesus did not say, "Why don't you have a little faith, or a mustard seed of faith, but He said, "Why don't you have *any* faith?" Jesus said, "I told y'all"… well, He probably didn't say y'all, but He did say, "I told you, let's go to the other side." In other words, if I told you, "Let's go to the other side," you can put your faith in the fact that I am going to get you to the other side.

Back on the ship headed to Tarshish, all the sailors were afraid of the huge storm, and each one cried out to their own god. They started throwing cargo over, while Jonah was asleep down below. The captain went down and told Jonah to get up and pray. Ironically, the sinner said to the preacher, "Get up and pray." They figured out Jonah was the cause of the storm because Jonah said, "It's me, it's me, it's me, oh Lord, standing in the need of prayer." No, I'm kidding, but Jonah did say "It's me, I am the one causing the storm." He told the sailors to throw him overboard. They asked for forgiveness and then threw him over.

Then *Jonah 1:17* says, *"But God provided a great fish..."* Isn't that just like God to swallow up all of our excuses and acts of disobedience in an effort to get us back on the right track? Jonah sat in the fish for three days, and then the Lord had the fish spit him out on dry land. Guess where the first piece of dry ground was located? That's right, Joppa, the port city where he made the choice to run. God had the big fish vomit him out at the *exact* place of his disobedience. So if you feel like you're always in the same place, guess what? You might want to do the last thing He told you to do so you can move forward. Covered in stomach bile, Jonah took off running in the right direction to preach an eight-word message to the city of Nineveh. *"Forty more days and Nineveh will be overturned"' (Jonah 3:4)*. The real miracle was that all the people in Nineveh repented and were saved. 2,500 people were saved. Talk about a revival! The king even demanded that all the animals repent and cover their heads in sackcloth. Can you imagine? What if I said to my little dog, "Okay, Annabelle, get on your knees and repent while I cover your head with sackcloth." She would be so scared, she would pee everywhere. Then I would have to repent for getting mad at Miss Pee-Pee Pants! Sometimes I practice my messages on my dogs, then have an altar call hoping my ten-year-old Yorkie, Zoe, will finally get saved. She can be pretty mean at times!

In *Jonah chapter 4*, the Word says Jonah was displeased and became angry. He told the Lord the reason he ran to Tarshish was because he knew God would forgive the people of Nineveh. He went on to ask God to take his life. He just couldn't bear to live if God was going to forgive Nineveh. He made himself a shelter, sat in its shade and waited to see what would happen to the city. Then the Lord provided a vine for Jonah so he would have better shade, but then He also provided a worm to eat the vine. Jonah was angry. God basically said, "Why are you concerned about a vine that popped up overnight that you did not make or tend to? You mean to tell Me, Jonah, you are happy when I'm taking care of you, but you're okay with 120,000 people of Nineveh, who don't know their right hand from their left, going to hell?"

You know, Peter did not have the faith Jesus would do what He said He would do, which was to return from the grave, but Jonah did have the faith God would do what He said He would do. Interestingly, the same faith made them both run. Stop sitting under your own tree, pouting because God forgave those who have hurt you when He has extended the same forgiveness to you for those you have hurt. Jonah is truly a "Cold Case Christian" because where we left him in chapter four, sitting under a tree, is exactly where God and the Bible left him. We don't hear what happened to him. Jonah was considered an "obese" Christian because he was full of the Word, but when it was time to share the good news, he did not want to spit out one morsel of hope to Nineveh. He would rather have stayed "obese" than offer hope to a dying generation. Many of us judge him for his behavior, but honestly, have we not done the same thing when God has asked us to forgive someone? We grab our running shoes and take off. We hand our ticket to the captain headed to Un-Forgiveness City, hiding below until God brings a storm in our lives that causes us to turn around. Jonah was made for more than just prophesying to people who would listen. He was made for more and saved for something. I'm sad to say, I don't think he ever realized his calling or reached his full potential in God.

If you enjoyed this chapter, please subscribe to my YouTube channel where I create three to five minute Vertical Hope videos. Search Michele Davenport with one "L."

Section One: Awareness of God's Presence

Faith Builder----What is something good God has done for you? An answer to prayer, a job opportunity, healing in your body, or maybe a financial breakthrough?

_____

_____

_____

Roadblocks----What roadblocks have presented themselves to you in a positive or negative way? How did you respond?

_____

_____

_____

Exits----Did you see any you needed to take during your week? Like for example, did you feel God was bidding you to exit a hurtful relationship? Or, maybe God was asking you to take an exit from your current job.

_____

_____

_____

Yield Signs----Were there any situations where you had the opportunity to take a purposeful pause before you reacted to someone or something?

_____

_____

_____

_____

Detours----Did you notice any detours God was trying to take you on? If so, what were they?

_____

_____

_____

_____

Shortcuts----Lastly, many times God will save us from repeating the same mistakes by taking us through a shortcut so we bypass the temptation. Did you recognize God moving like this in your life this week? If so, how?

_____

_____

_____

_____

Section Two: Practical Life Application

Fill in the blank:

"The _____ of the Lord came to Jonah, go to the great city of Nineveh and_____ against it, because its _____ has come up before me." Jonah 1:1-2

Has God ever called you to do something, and your first reaction was to run from the call?

_____

If so, did you ever accomplish what He asked you to do? What was the outcome?

_____

_____

_____

_____

When a storm comes in your life, what do you think of first?

_____

_____

_____

_____

Have you ever considered the storm to be a provision from God instead of something Satan created?

_____

What was the last storm you had in your life?

_____

_____

_____

What did you learn from the experience? On a scale from 1-10, 10 being the highest level of faith, where was your faith during the storm?

_____

_____

_____

_____

Chapter Ten

The Good Samaritan

". . . A man was going down from Jerusalem to Jericho, when he fell into the hands of robbers. They stripped him of his clothes, beat him and went away, leaving him half dead. A priest happened to be going down the same road, and when he saw the man, he passed on the other side. So too, a Levite, when he came to the place and saw him, passed on the other side. But a Samaritan, as he traveled, came where the man was; and when he saw him, he took pity on him. He went to him and bandaged his wounds, pouring on oil and wine. Then he put the man on his own donkey, took him to an inn and took care of him. The next day he took out two silver coins and gave them to the innkeeper. Look after him, he said, and when I return, I will reimburse you for any extra expense you may have."
Luke 10:30-35

It's amazing! In light of this new and increasingly convincing evidence, unknown causes of "spiritual death" are being determined, and "Cold Case Christian" files are finally being cracked. Surprisingly, as I was investigating the third and last case, I found you and me in the files.

Third Case: The Priest and the Levite (of The Good Samaritan Parable)

Crime Scene: The Book of Luke

Cause of Death: Spiritual Anorexia

Evidence: Torn t-shirt, oil, and wine

Definition of "Spiritual Anorexia": condition found in Christians who never really eat the Word of God, the will of God, or the promises of God. They are only living to die, all the while living a non-purpose driven life.

In *Luke 10:25-37*, an expert of the law asked what he must do to inherit eternal life? Jesus replied, *"'What does the law say, how do you read it?' He answered, 'Love the Lord your God with all your heart and with all your soul and with all your strength and with all your mind and love your neighbor as yourself.' Jesus said, 'You have answered correctly, do this and you will live.' But the expert of the law wanted to justify himself, so he asked Jesus, 'And who is my neighbor?'"* In answer to his question, Jesus told him the *parable of the Good Samaritan*. It was the man left beaten and half naked in the ditch. You know, the more I investigated this case, the more I found you and me in between the pages of Luke. The truth is we were all "cold case anorexic believers," or non-believers, running around with no spiritual food to eat.

Allow me a few more minutes of your time to make my case. Let's start with some facts. There was a man, a Jew perhaps, beaten almost to death and left naked in a ditch on the side of the road. An "anorexic" priest passed by on the other side. An "anorexic" Levite passed by on the other side. But, a Samaritan took pity on him. He was moved with compassion and bandaged the beaten man's wounds while pouring oil and wine on him. I doubt the Good Samaritan had a first-aid kit on him. I believe he literally tore his own clothes to bandage him. Also the Word said he poured out oil and wine on his wounds, loaded his neighbor on his own donkey and took him to an inn where he paid for the man to stay. When left to himself, an "anorexic" Christian walks on the other side of the Word. Listen y'all, until Jesus, like the Good Samaritan, showed up on the scene of our lives, crossing the road between heaven and earth, we were all "anorexic cold cases" bound to hell with no purpose to fulfill. He poured out the oil (the Holy Spirit) on us and covered us with the wine (His Blood). His clothes were torn. Then He wrapped our wounds and helped us heal. He clothed us with His righteousness and paid the final price to allow us into the inn (Heaven). You were made for more and saved for something!

At what point in our lives do we stop faking it until we make it? When are we going to make a life decision to really be alive in Christ? If we just go around being complacent, if we're not careful we will end up in a spiritual morgue with a toe tag labeled either "Bulimic Jane Doe," "Obese Jane Doe," or "Anorexic Jane Doe." Jesus said to the church in Sardis, "You look alive but you are dead. You do all these deeds, but you have a spiritual disorder."

"Bulimic Christian" Peter could not find enough faith that Jesus would do what He said He would do. So, Peter went back to his old habit, purging out the truth for a lie. The whole purpose for Peter's life was to feed the sheep. Jesus stood on the shore of Galilee wooing Peter back from fishing, refocusing Peter on the call on his life. After his encounter with Jesus, Peter was off and running to accomplish what Jesus had established for him to do. He was made for more and saved for something besides fishing for fish. His purpose was to go, to go feed the sheep, preach the Word and lead people to Jesus. Three-thousand got saved when he preached his first message. Five thousand got saved on another occasion. People would just walk by Peter's shadow and get healed. It has been noted by scholars, even while Peter was in a horrific jail before his death, Peter got the jailer saved along with 47 others. Your old habit will keep you out of the will and purpose of God in your life. You are a new creation in Christ. Peter tried to take a shortcut and ended back where he started, Galilee. It's not over. It's not finished. You hang on!

The "Obese Christian," Jonah, did have the faith God would do what He said He would do. Jonah just did not want Him to. So Jonah wanted to hoard up the truth that Nineveh's repentance would lead to their forgiveness. He wanted them dead. He wanted them to pay for their sin. Where is Jonah? Still pouting in chapter four, that's where the Bible left him, and that's where God left him. Jonah is truly a "cold case;" we never hear anything else about Jonah. Un-forgiveness will keep you from the will and purpose of God. It will develop a root of bitterness that strangles out every good thing.

"Anorexic Christians," like the priest and Levite, really don't understand who the Good Samaritan is. They don't eat the food of God. Not knowing who you are in Christ, and who Christ is in you, will keep you from the will and purpose of God in your life.

John 4:34, "My food is to do the will of God and to finish the work."

Ephesians 2:10, "For we are God's workmanship, created in Christ Jesus to do good works, which God prepared in advance for us to do."

The "cold cases" are all solved; there is nothing else to do. I am not a "spiritual cold case." No, I am the opposite. The case I'm building is for the kingdom of God. My file is full of evidence of how my God still heals, delivers, restores, redirects, redeems, reunites and rehabilitates His relationship with His children. He is not done, it's not over, He is not finished! I challenge you to build your case for Christ one answered prayer at a time.

If you enjoyed this chapter, please subscribe to my YouTube channel where I create three to five minute Vertical Hope videos. Search Michele Davenport with one "L."

Section One: Awareness of God's Presence

Faith Builder----What is something good God has done for you? An answer to prayer, a job opportunity, healing in your body, or maybe a financial breakthrough?

_____

_____

_____

_____

Roadblocks----What roadblocks have presented themselves to you in a positive or negative way? How did you respond?

_____

_____

_____

_____

Exits----Did you see any you needed to take during your week? Like for example, did you feel God was bidding you to exit a hurtful relationship? Or, maybe God was asking you to take an exit from your current job.

_____

_____

_____

_____

Yield Signs----Were there any situations where you had the opportunity to take a purposeful pause before you reacted to someone or something?

_____

_____

_____

Detours----Did you notice any detours God was trying to take you on? If so, what were they?

_____

_____

_____

_____

Shortcuts----Lastly, many times God will save us from repeating the same mistakes by taking us through a shortcut so we bypass the temptation. Did you recognize God moving like this in your life this week? If so, how?

_____

_____

_____

_____

Section Two: Practical Life Application

When was the last time you did something to love your neighbor? What did you do?

_____

_____

_____

Who do you consider your neighbor?

What were you created to do?

What are you doing to finish the work you were created to do?

What's in your evidence file for God?

_____

_____

Challenge:

Get a box. Decorate it by yourself, or if you have kids, let them help. Label the box "Answered Prayers." Throughout the year, every time God answers one of your prayers, big or small, write it down and place it in the box. Around Thanksgiving, get out your box and read them as you stand in complete thankfulness for God's mercy and power.

Chapter Eleven

Made for More and Saved for Something

"You intended to harm me, but God intended it for good to accomplish what is now being done, the saving of many lives." Genesis 50:20

Moses was born at a time when Pharaoh was getting a little paranoid because the Hebrews were growing in numbers, and Pharaoh thought they would rebel and run away. So, he wanted the midwives to kill all the Hebrew newborn baby boys. You see, what Pharaoh didn't understand was God made Moses for more and saved him for something. Let's take a final journey together to see how we can relate Moses' life to our own. Watch how God uses even the bad to bring about good. Moses was born with a purpose and a plan, which God placed on his life before he was in his mother's womb. You and I are born with a God purpose and plan on our lives as well. One of Moses' purposes in life was to deliver the Hebrews out of slavery.

I'm not sure how much you remember about the story of Moses, but here's a little synopsis. Moses' mother went to great lengths to keep him safe for three months after he was born because Pharaoh had issued the order to kill all the Hebrew boys who were born. But there came a time when she couldn't keep him quiet any longer, so she put him in a papyrus basket covered in pitch, placed him in the Nile river, gave him a push, and into the reeds he went. Oh, the tears that must have flowed down her cheeks that day as she quietly cried in despair, wondering if she would ever see her son again. As she watched him drift away, I could only imagine the grief she felt. It must have seemed as if she was placing Moses into a river tomb. As her heart was wrenched with intense emotions, she clinched her hands tightly and restrained herself from retrieving Moses out of the Nile. The questions she must have pondered. *What if no one sees him? What if he drowns or starves to death? What if the wrong person finds him and kills him anyway?* I'm sure she was consumed with many doubts and concerns, but she placed him in the Nile, taking the chance that he would live.

Just as God would have it, Pharaoh's daughter went down to the Nile to bathe. As she walked along the river banks, she saw a basket in the reeds. Pharaoh's daughter sent her slave girl to retrieve the basket. She opened it and saw the baby. Maybe he was crying, maybe not. But either way, she felt sorry for him. She immediately knew this was one of the Hebrew babies. In that very moment, we see God working out what the enemy meant for harm. God was turning it all around for the good. Watch this—I don't want you to miss even a minute of the miracle. Moses' sister was on the sidelines watching all this happen. She hollered down to Pharaoh's daughter, "Shall I go get one of the Hebrew women to nurse the baby for you?" She said, "Yes, go!" His sister went and got their mother. Did you catch that? Wow! Pharaoh's daughter said to Moses' mother, "Take this baby and nurse him for me, and I will pay you." Moses' mother took him and nursed him. When Moses became older, she took him back to Pharaoh's daughter, and he became her son. She named him Moses, saying, "I drew him out of the Nile."

Many years had passed, and Moses was grown now. One day he was walking where his people, the Israelites, were working. He turned around and saw an Egyptian beating one of his own. Moses glanced this way and that way, then he killed the Egyptian and hid his body in the sand. The next day, he went out and saw two Hebrew men hitting each other. He said, "Why are you hitting your fellow Hebrew?" One of the men said, "Who made you ruler over us? Are you thinking about killing me as you killed the Egyptian?" Then Moses was afraid. He realized what he had done must have been discovered. Pharaoh caught wind of the incident and tried to kill Moses, so Moses fled to Midian.

As he was sitting by a well, seven sisters came up to the well to fetch some water, but some shepherds came and tried to run the women off. Moses rescued them. After the sisters returned home, they told their father what had happened and how Moses had saved them from the shepherds. The father said, "Go, invite him to eat with us." The father asked Moses to stay with them, and he gave Moses his daughter, Zipporah, as his wife. Moses and Zipporah had a son and named him Gershom.

After a long period of time, the king of Egypt died. The Israelites cried out in anguish to God. They were tired of being slaves, starving to death and living in terrible conditions. Their clothes hadn't been washed in years, the baths were few and far between, the meals, if any, were scraps at best. Their bones were protruding from their skin, their children cried from hunger, and they lived in their own filth. Every muscle in their bodies ached from being abused. Every bone cried out in desperation for relief. The life they had was diminishing, their hope was falling, and joy was a thing of the past. Everyday looked the same as the day before. The only difference might have been the quota of bricks they were expected to make for the day they were facing. God heard their cries and was concerned for them.

As Moses was leading the flock on the back side of a mountain called Horeb, which means, "desolate region," something on that particular day was different. There was a burning bush that would not be consumed. This was a bush he might have seen and walked by a hundred times, but that day, it was on fire and the flame would not be put out. Moses was captivated by the bush, so he walked over to see the strange sight. I can only imagine what he might have been thinking. As he slowly approached the bush, did he wonder what kept it from being consumed?

As I was reading in Exodus about Moses and the burning bush, I couldn't help but process in the realm of types and shadows. Could this all-consuming fire represent hell, the fire that never goes out and the hell the Israelites were living in because the Egyptians kept them in bondage? Was God using this story in a far more intellectual way than we first observed by reading it as a Bible story? Could it be Moses represents Christ, and the burning bush represents the fiery hell we were all doomed to before Christ? Did Mt. Horeb represent the desolate place we all once occupied until we met our Savior, Jesus? Does the enslavement of the Israelites by the Egyptians represent the enslavement by the enemy with his lies and deceit? My mind couldn't help but go there. If this is too far-fetched for you, that's okay, you can catch up when I reel myself back in!

When the Lord saw Moses at the bush, He called to him from within the bush, "'Moses! Moses!'" Moses said, "'Here I am.'" God said, "'Do not come any closer, take off your sandals, for the place you are standing on is holy ground.'"

I've gleaned many truths from this story, but one truth I can plainly see is God knows where you are. He knows if you're on the back side of a mountain tending to the flock, or if you're in a cubicle in an office on the fifth floor. God knows what house you live in and where you shop for groceries. God has not misplaced you. Moses was just doing his normal flock-tending, something he had done for forty years. That is until he saw something he was not prepared to see and heard something he was not prepared to hear. God was speaking from the bush. He said, "Take off your sandals for the place you are standing on is holy ground." In other words, "Take off the sandals that walked through the dirt and dust you chose to walk through. I'm calling you from your past into your future, a future I created for you to walk in. You were made for more and saved for something, Moses. Now, My son, you are standing on My ground. I'm calling you to the uncommon. I'm using the most unlikely to accomplish the most important."

Take off the shoes of your past. I'm telling you, y'all, your past does not disqualify you. You were who you were before God called you. Moses was still Moses. He was still a murderer hiding behind a mountain, but God chose to use him even though he had a past. He had sinned. He was not perfect, and he was hiding out and hoping not to be seen or recognized. Moses was made for more and saved for something… and so are you. It's time, y'all. Take off the past, forgive what needs to be forgiven, give grace where you need to give grace, restore what needs restoration, and get ready for God to use you. He is about to do a new thing in your life, but you can't take those old shoes with you. The shoes may represent an old way of thinking, a way of life, a concept, a negative seed that was sown in you long ago, an old image, or who you were before Christ was real to you. Remove the hindrances in your life. God has a plan. Too often we settle for Plan B because we don't have the faith for Plan A. Are you ready for a change, a change that requires Plan A faith?

Now, I've walked you through many stories throughout the Bible showing you how God has chosen to work through Biblical people. I have given a brief testimony of how God restored and renewed my life through His grace and mercy. I shared with you how His design for me overshadowed my past abuse and addictions. Your life matters, and God created you in His image. You were made for more and saved for something, just as Moses was. God could not allow Moses to live the rest of his days tending to the flock when He had a purpose far greater for Moses to accomplish. He loved Moses enough to start a fire that could not be consumed and wooed Moses back to his calling. His mistakes may have delayed his purpose, but it did not void his calling. God still has a calling on your life. You were made for more and saved for something.

As for Peter, who we also studied, he too, was made for more and saved for something. Jesus did not allow Peter to fade away on the banks of Galilee. He wooed him back as well. Jesus loved Peter enough not allow him to return to his old habit, because he was made for more and saved for something. Remember, after his restorative encounter with Jesus, people walking by Peter's shadow were healed and three thousand were saved when he preached his first message. Peter made a difference while he walked the earth because he accepted and acknowledged the concept that he was made for more and saved for something other than just being a fisherman. Oh, don't misunderstand me… I'm not suggesting his occupation wasn't important, because God used it. What I'm saying is that Peter was made for more and saved for something other than his occupation, and so are you. What you do isn't who you are. You may style hair, but you ARE a child of God. You may practice medicine, but you ARE a child of God. Or you may teach for a living, but you ARE a child of God with a God-given purpose and plan for your life.

The Good Samaritan stopped and helped a Jew. He went out of his way to be an answer to someone else's prayer when others just walked by to leave the half-naked and beaten man to die in ditch. I can't help but think his actions that day revealed that the Good Samaritan knew he was made for more and saved for something. People who truly grasp their relevance in life do uncommon things. They don't live by the norm but are the "abnormal" people of this world, a bit unusual, but fascinating as well, because their faith overrides their fear and propels them to do what God has designed them to do.

A while back, I met a friend at Starbucks. As we were sitting there talking, a lady walked across the parking lot with her hands full, and she dropped her keys. I thought for a moment I should get up and retrieve her keys, but in the time it took me to have the thought, she had already picked them up. My attention was then back on my conversation with Abby. As we finished visiting and were about to wrap up our girl time, Abby said she had a word for me. She asked if I noticed the huge tropical parrot on the lady's arm (the lady who dropped her keys). I said, "No." Abby said, "Michele, you're like a tropical parrot." I looked at her with a bit of confusion. She said, "How unusual is it to see a tropical parrot, in Missouri, at a Starbucks?" She went on to say, "You are like that parrot. You are unusual and you stand out, but don't change!" She said she thought I was called to our church to challenge others to do the same.

This was the second time I had been told something to this effect. My friend, Pam, heard a song by Francesca Battistelli called *Unusual*. She said when she heard this song, it reminded her of me. One of the lines in the song is, "You're the zebra in the pony show." Ha ha ha! Sometimes I feel like I'm a zebra walking around Missouri, a little bit out of place. The Word of God says I'm *in* the world, but I'm not *of* the world. You know, I can live with that.

You see, I don't mind being referred to as unusual because I know what that means. It means I was made for more and saved for something. I will not settle for anything less than what God has planned for me and my life. I will not allow my past to dictate my future or stomp out my growth in the Lord. I will not look back with a heart of un-forgiveness, bitterness, or even envy over what could have been different, because I know everything the enemy means for harm, God works out for good. But it's up to me to recognize this piece of truth in my life. God has used my mistakes, as well as my successes, to bring Him glory. What God has *not* used is any of my complacency.

It's sad because when I studied Jonah, I knew he was made or more and saved for something, but he did not embrace it. He settled in and became complacent in his calling. He was a prophet, but he was made for more. He was supposed to bring the Good News to Nineveh, which he eventually did. He was a prophet who did not want to prophesy. He wanted 120,000 people to die. Although Jonah was made for more, he was left in Jonah chapter four, pouting over God forgiving Nineveh's people. He wanted forgiveness for his sins, but he didn't want a select group to be forgiven for theirs. Some of you are living in the same realm of thinking right now. You mess up and you ask God to forgive you, but you don't want that person who hurt you to be forgiven. You might be thinking, *Michele, I do want them forgiven.* Yes, you might want *God* to forgive them, but *you're* sure not going to forgive them. My friend, that's a "Jonah spirit" right there. You were made for more and saved for something. Go ahead and forgive others freely, just as you have been forgiven.

Remember the woman with the issue of blood in chapter two? This is an example of a woman who knew she was made for more and saved for something. She had suffered for twelve years with an issue of blood. The Word said she had spent all she had on the remedies of this world but to no avail. She was not only still sick, but she had spent all her money on doctors too. I admire her a lot because she was willing to risk it all just to touch the hem of Jesus' garment. I believe she realized she was made for more and saved for something. The moment you realize this truth in your own life is the moment that you will do the uncommon. The Word said she overheard people talking about Jesus. I think in that "overhearing" she received a revelation about her value. No longer was she willing to hand out money to doctors who could not help her. No longer was she satisfied with being an outcast to society or being shut out of the temple and considered unclean. No, she rose up and gathered her faith to become who God created her to be. As she crawled through the crowd, she whispered, "If I can but touch the hem of His garment, I will be made whole." I can almost hear her saying, "Oh no, devil, I was made for more and saved for something. Get out of my way. I'm fixing to be made whole. I will not spend one more day with an issue of blood, one more hour in defeat, or one more minute being considered unclean due to my condition. You better move over and make way, because I've gotten a hold of truth, and I'm ready to start living my life." Will you say that today? Will you agree that you were made for more and saved for something? You'd better wake up tomorrow morning and tell the devil to move on, because you are not going to settle for common any longer. From this day forward, you are going to live an uncommon life with a real big God!

You were created with something inside of you, something God put there. Some of you know what I'm talking about, but there are others who don't have a clue. You know, Adam had Eve inside of him the whole time. Adam didn't know he had Eve inside of him until God pulled her out. Did you hear me? Eve was in Adam all along. God pulled her from his rib. Adam, in a perfect garden without sin, at his best, still had more in him that he was not even aware of. I'm telling you, and I'm telling me, that we haven't tapped into all God has put in us yet. We were made for more and saved for something!

Mary was made for more than just to be married to Joseph. She was made to give birth to Jesus. Jesus was in her, but until she gave birth to Him, no one could see the power inside her. Some of you just need to give birth to what God has already supernaturally impregnated you with.

I didn't know I could write poetry until my dad died, and God pulled it out of me. I didn't realize I was a writer until God pulled it out of me through grief in my thirties. I didn't know I was a leader and speaker until my mid-thirties when God pulled it out of me. I didn't know I had a CEO of a ministry inside of me, but God did. I was made for more, but until I allowed the pulling process to bring out of me what God had placed in me, I would have continued to live beneath my potential.

Abraham had a whole nation in him. That's kind of impressive! Sarah had a baby in her in her nineties. Noah had the ability to build an ark and save his whole family to repopulate the entire world inside of him. David had a king in him. He also had a fighter, in him, one who killed Goliath. Gideon had a mighty man of valor in him. Ruth had a huge amount of courage in her. Job had patience and endurance in him. Hannah had a miracle child in her who came to her through prayer. The woman with the issue of blood had her healing living inside her. Esther had a queen in her who saved an entire nation. Deborah had a judge and warrior in her. Joshua had an overcomer in him who led the Israelites across the Jordan into the Promised Land. Elijah had resurrection power in him and saved a widow woman and her son from certain death. John the Baptist had a spokesman for Jesus in him.

There were forty authors of the Bible, forty people who had the Bible inside them and were responsible for the 66 books that make up our Bible today. What did all these people have in common? They all had it in them all along, but God had to pull it out. The question I leave with you today is "What is in you that you have not allowed God to pull out and use?"

You were Made for More and Saved for Something, and the day you grasp this piece of truth, you will do uncommon things for the glory of God who created you with more in mind!

If you enjoyed this chapter, please subscribe to my YouTube channel where I create three to five minute Vertical Hope videos. Search Michele Davenport with one "L."

Section One: Awareness of God's Presence

Faith Builder----What is something good God has done for you? An answer to prayer, a job opportunity, healing in your body, or maybe a financial breakthrough?

_____

_____

_____

_____

Roadblocks----What roadblocks have presented themselves to you in a positive or negative way? How did you respond?

_____

_____

_____

_____

Exits----Did you see any you needed to take during your week? Like for example, did you feel God was bidding you to exit a hurtful relationship? Or, maybe God was asking you to take an exit from your current job.

_____

_____

_____

_____

Yield Signs----Were there any situations where you had the opportunity to take a purposeful pause before you reacted to someone or something?

_____

_____

_____

_____

Detours----Did you notice any detours God was trying to take you on? If so, what were they?

_____

_____

_____

_____

Shortcuts----Lastly, many times God will save us from repeating the same mistakes by taking us through a shortcut so we bypass the temptation. Did you recognize God moving like this in your life this week? If so, how?

_____

_____

_____

_____

Section Two: Practical Life Application

Have you ever had to trust God in a life and death situation? If so, explain.

_____

_____

_____

_____

Have you felt like God told you to take off your shoes, to take off your past, because He wanted to do a new thing, but first you had to let go of the old? Did you obey? What did you do?

_____

_____

_____

_____

Do you believe you were Made for More and Saved for Something?

_____

What do you think you're saved for? What's your gifting?

_____

_____

_____

_____

What chapter or story ministered to you the most and why?

_____

_____

_____

_____

Who are you in Christ?

_____

_____

_____

_____

Challenge:

Ask someone you trust to tell you what they see as your primary gifting. After you receive their answer, go to God and ask Him how you can use what He has placed in you to bless others

References:

Chapter One
Isaiah 61:10 (NIV)
2 Corinthians 5:17 (NIV)

Chapter Two
Maximized Manhood by Ed Cole
Heart Transplant information: www.secondscount.org

Chapter Three
Strong's Concordance
Vine's Expository Dictionary
1 Kings 18-19 (NIV)
Abraham: Genesis 11-25 (NIV)
2 Corinthians 2:11 (NIV)
John 8:44 (NIV)
2 Corinthians 5:17 (NIV)
1Peter 5:8 (NIV)

Chapter Four
African impala story: http://www.theexeterdaily.co.uk/
Strong's Concordance
Vine's Expository Dictionary
Noah: Genesis 6-7 (NIV)
Ezekiel: Ezekiel 37:1-14 (NIV)
Woman with the issue of blood: Mark 5:25-34 (NIV)
Moses: Exodus 3-14 (NIV)
Joshua: Joshua 3-4 (NIV)
Jesus: Matthew 26-28; Mark 14-16; Luke 22-24; John 18-20 (NIV)
Abraham: Genesis 22 (NIV)

Chapter Five
Joseph: Genesis 30-50 (NIV)
Job: Book of Job (NIV)
Abraham: Genesis 11-25 (NIV)
Jacob and Esau: Genesis 25:19-34 (NIV)
Genesis 17:15 (NIV)
Genesis 17:5 (NIV)
Acts 13:9 (NIV)

Chapter Six
Leviticus 20:10 (NIV)
John 8:4-11 (NIV)
John 11:1-44 (NIV)
Matthew 1:25 (NIV)

Chapter Seven
Strong's Concordance
Vine's Expository Dictionary
Jabez's prayer: 1 Chronicles 4:10 (NIV)

Chapter Eight
Webster's Dictionary
Romans 6:11 (NIV)
Strong's Concordance
Vine's Expository Dictionary
The Great Commission: Matthew 28:19-20 (NIV)

Chapter Nine
James 1:22 (NIV)
Jonah 1:1-17 (NIV) Jonah 2:10 (NIV)
Jonah 4:1-11 (NIV)

Chapter Ten
Revelations 3:1 (NIV)
2 Corinthians 5:17 (NIV)

Chapter Eleven
1 Corinthians 1:27-29 (NIV)
Isaiah 43:19 (NIV)
John 17:14-15 (NIV)
Ephesians 4:32 (NIV)
Adam: Genesis 2:21-23 (NIV)
Mary: Matthew 1; Luke 1-2 (NIV)
Abraham: Genesis 12:2-3 (NIV)
Sarah: Genesis 17:16-17, 21:1-2 (NIV)
Moses: Exodus 2-3 (NIV)
Noah: Genesis 6-7 (NIV)
David: 1Samuel 17 (NIV)
Gideon: Judges 6:12 (NIV)
Ruth: Book of Ruth (NIV)
Job: Book of Job (NIV)
Hannah: 1 Samuel 1:27-28 (NIV)
Woman with the issue of blood: Mark 5:25-34 (NIV)
Esther: Book of Esther (NIV)
Deborah: Judges 4-5 (NIV)
Joshua: Joshua 3-4 (NIV)
Elijah: 1 Kings 17 (NIV)
John the Baptist: Mark 1:2-3 (NIV)

Salvation Prayer

If you haven't given your life to Christ yet, and you want to, just say this simple prayer with me, and you will surely be saved.

Lord Jesus, I know I am sinner. You sent Your Son to the cross for me, to be beaten, mocked and crucified. I'm confessing with my mouth and believing in my heart that You are Lord. I believe Your Son went to the grave and You raised Him from death, so I could be saved. Thank You, Lord, for Your grace and mercy upon my life. Amen.

"If you confess with your mouth, Jesus is Lord, and believe in your heart that God raised him from the dead, you will be saved." Romans 10:9

If you repeated this simple prayer, I want you to write the date down so you can remember your new birthdate. According to Scripture, we all must be born again to enter the kingdom of heaven.

"Jesus replied, "Very truly I tell you, no one can see the kingdom of God unless they are born again." John 3:3

I want to leave you with some Vertical Hope Scriptures that say who you are in Christ. It's time you take back what the enemy has tried to steal and start living out your potential, because you, my friend, were... come on, say it with me... Made for More and Saved for Something!

"Who I am in Christ" Scriptures:

1. A child of God (Rom. 8:16)
2. Saved by grace through faith (Eph. 2:8)
3. Sanctified (Heb.13:12)
4. Redeemed from the curse of the law (Gal. 3:13)
5. The temple of the Holy Spirit (1 Cor. 6:19)
6. Led by the Spirit of God (Rom. 8:14)
7. A saint (Rom. 1:7)
8. Kept in safety wherever I go (Ps. 91:10-11)
9. Strong in the Lord and the power of His might (Eph. 6:10)
10. Able to do all things through Christ who strengthens me (Phil. 4:13)
11. An heir of God and joint heir with Jesus (Rom. 8:17)
12. Holy and without blame before Him (1 Pet. 1:16)
13. Sealed with Holy Spirit of promise (Eph. 1:13)
14. Accepted in the beloved (Eph. 1:13)
15. Crucified with Christ (Gal. 2:20)
16. Free from condemnation (Rom. 8:1)
17. Blessed through obedience (Deut. 28:1)
18. An heir of eternal life (1 John 5:11,12)
19. Healed by His stripes (1 Peter 2:24)
20. Above only and not beneath (Deut. 28:13)
21. Empowered to establish God's Word here on earth (Matt.16:19)
22. An overcomer by the word of my testimony (Rev. 12:11)
23. Firmly rooted-built up and established in my faith (Col. 2:7)
24. Circumcised in the Spirit (Col. 2:11)
25. Bold in the world (1 John 4:17)
26. Born of God and the evil one does not touch me (1 John 5:18)
27. His disciple because I have love for others (John 13:34, 35)

28. Not moved by what I see (2 Cor. 4:18)
29. Able to cast down vein imaginations (2 Cor. 10:4,5)
30. Being transformed by the renewing of my mind (Rom. 12:1,2)
31. The righteousness of God in Christ (2 Cor. 5:21)
32. The light of the world (Matt. 5:14)
33. Dead to sin but alive unto righteousness (1 Pet. 2:24)
34. An ambassador for Christ (2 Cor. 5:20)
35. God's workmanship created in Christ Jesus (Eph. 2:10)
36. Created in God's image (Gen. 1:26)
37. I am very good (Gen. 1:31)
38. Raised up with Christ and seated in heavenly places (Col. 2:12)
39. Fearfully and wonderfully made (Ps.139:14)
40. A slave of righteousness (Rom. 6:18)
41. Chosen and appointed by Christ to bear His fruit (John 15:16)
42. United to the Lord and one spirit with Him (1 Cor. 6:17)
43. A son of God and one in Christ (Gal. 3:26,28)
44. A son of light and not darkness (1 Thes. 5:5)
45. Chosen of God, holy and beloved (Col. 3:12)
46. An expression of the life of Christ-He is my life (Col. 3:4)
47. An alien and stranger to this temporary world (1 Pet. 2:11)
48. A living stone, being built up in Christ as a spiritual house (1Pet. 2:5)
49. A member of a chosen race, a royal priesthood, a holy nation,
50. God's special possession (1 Pet. 2:9,10)
51. Forgiven (Col. 1:13,14)
52. Justified (Rom. 5:1)
53. Redeemed from the hand of the enemy (Ps. 107:2)
54. A new creature (2 Cor. 5:17)
55. Delivered from the power of darkness (Col. 1:13)
56. A son of God (Rom. 8:14)
57. The head and not the tail (Deut. 28:13)
58. Getting all my needs met by Jesus (Phil. 4:19)
59. Able to cast all my cares on Jesus (1 Pet. 5:7)
60. Set free (John 8:31-33)
61. Heir to the blessing of Abraham (Gal. 3:13,14)
62. Victorious (Rev. 21:7)
63. A partaker of Christ, I share His life (Heb. 3:14)
64. Complete in Him (Col. 2:10)

65. Alive in Christ (Eph.2:5)
66. Reconciled to God (2 Cor. 5:18)
67. Blessed coming in and blessed going out (Deut. 28:6)
68. Blessed with all spiritual blessings (Eph. 1:3)
69. Able to exercise my authority over the enemy (Luke 10:9)
70. More than a conqueror (Rom. 8:37)
71. An overcomer by the blood of the lamb (Rev. 12:11)
72. Able to daily overcome the devil (1 John 4:4)
73. A fellow citizen with the saints (Eph. 2:19)
74. Built upon the foundation of Jesus (Eph. 2:20)
75. His faithful follower (Eph. 5:1)
76. The salt of the earth (Matt. 5:13)
77. Called of God (2 Tim. 1:9)
78. Walking by faith not by sight (2 Cor. 5:7)
79. Able to bring every thought into captivity (2 Cor. 10:5)
80. A laborer together with God (1Cor. 3:9)
81. An imitator of Jesus (Eph. 5:1)
82. Blessing the Lord at all times (Ps. 34:1)
83. Chosen (1 Thes. 1:4)
84. The apple of my Father's eye (Deut. 32:10)
85. Being changed into His image (2 Cor. 3:18)
86. Beloved of God (Col. 3:12)
87. One in Christ (John 17:21-23)
88. Christ's friend (John 15:15)
89. Enslaved to God (Rom. 6:22)
90. Will resemble Christ when He returns (1 John 3:1,2)
91. A branch of the true vine, a channel of Christ's life (John 15:1,5)
92. Hidden with Christ in God (Col. 3:3)
93. A member of Christ's body (1 Cor. 12:27, Eph. 5:30)
94. A holy partaker of a heavenly calling (Heb. 3:1)
95. An enemy of the devil (1Pet. 5:8)
96. Loved (Jer. 31:3)
97. Radiant (Ps. 34:5)
98. Purified (1 John 1:9)
99. Strong (Isa. 40:29-31)
100. Valuable (Luke 12:24)
101. Celebrated (Zeph. 3:17)

Walking a walk worth repeating.

I'm dipping my toe in the Jordan, expecting a miracle.

Michele Davenport, President/CEO of Faith Builders Ministries, is available for speaking engagements at your church or women's event.

Contact Info:

Phone: 817-797-2105

Website: fbministries.com

Please feel free to connect with her on Facebook at Faith Builders Ministries, Inc. or through Instagram at faithbuilders_ministries

Please enjoy a few chapters from three of the other books Michele has written.

The first one, *Ripened on the Vine,* is a true story of Michele's life as she endured emotional, physical, mental and sexual abuse in her past. Walk with her as she learned how to find her vertical hope in a horizontal world. The book is really not about her, but more about the One who created her and saved her from death so many times.

RIPENED ON THE VINE

Lori Michele Davenport

<u>Chapter One</u>

The Seed in Me

I'm like a flower, and You planted the seed . . .
You were watching me grow into becoming me . . .
Making mistakes along the way . . .
Struggling to hear what my Father has to say . . .
Closing my eyes and searching my heart . . .
Finding the place where I needed to start . . .
At the beginning is a good place to be,
but in the middle is where you will find me . . .
I'm like a flower and You planted the seed . . .

Hello, my name is Michele. I dedicate my story to anyone who has ever had a reason to give up on life and God. My heart's desire is for people to be encouraged, not by my life, but by what God has done through my life. This book is not about me. It is about the One who created me, and saved me from death so many times. I once heard a preacher, Myles Munroe, say, "God salvages (saves) people and puts them back together so He can use them for what He originally planned on using them for."

What I was born to do caused God to save me. God has a plan for all of us, and He will save you, too. God has revealed to me that my childhood and my life have been *faith builders*. He has used them to strengthen my faith in Him.

144

Lord God, please guide my hands and heart as I begin to tell my life story to all who need a little faith. Thank You, Lord, for never leaving me alone, for being faithful in salvaging me to glorify You.

The last two years of their marriage, my dad began to drink a lot. I was in bed sleeping when I was awakened by a loud noise. I wasn't sure what it was. I saw my dad's face. He got me out of bed. My brother wasn't there that evening. He was at my uncle's house where my dad was staying because my parents were separated. My dad took me into the living room where I saw the front door lying in the middle of the room. He had kicked it completely down. He sat me in the corner while I watched him abuse my mother. I was only 4 years old, and that was the earliest memory of my dad. It was the only one that I would have for a long time. I cannot possibly tell you the impression, the visions, the distorted idea of love that was embedded in my mind that night. I was so young and all I could think was that my dad was trying to kill my mom.

Throughout their marriage, he beat her, fooled around with other women and continually assaulted her self-worth. After he left that evening, my mom found the strength to call my grandmother. She came and picked us up and took us to the hospital. My mom was so badly beaten that the doctors did not know if my mom would live. The state attorney's representative came by to take my mom's statement, but she had slipped into a coma. Her neck looked like she had been strangled, and since she was in a coma, they could not get all the facts. Later, they found out that my dad did this with his bare hands. The officers could not believe the damage he had done. I do not remember how long my mom was in the hospital, but after my mom got out, we went to live with my grandma. We had to pass that apartment every day and I would say, "That is where it happened, Mom, isn't it?" The memories of what happened were strong in my mind, and I did not want to be around my dad.

When my brother found out what had happened to mom, he begged her to drop the charges, and my mom did. Soon after this happened, my dad checked into a mental hospital. Later we found out why my dad decided to have this last revenge on our mother. He found out the divorce would be final in six days, and that was more than he could stand. He went insane that night. After dad got out of the mental hospital, he disappeared in Corpus Christi to hide from paying child support and the police. While in Corpus, he met his future wife. She seemed to keep my dad out of trouble. My parents had married young and divorced young. The first two years of their marriage, dad got put into prison for burglary. My dad was not a very nice man back then.

Before the divorce, my brother and I used to pray that God would save their marriage. After that night, we prayed that He would never answer that prayer. God has His hands on our lives even before we know Him. When we pray, and we do not think God has answered our prayers, know that He is God and we might not receive the answer we expect, but He gives the answer that is best for us.

As I'm typing this story, I have an amazing chill. Not because of the pain I felt back then, but because of the healing I feel now, and the peace I have with my dad and my mom. The emptiness that followed in the years to come was overwhelming at times. I did not realize how important a father figure in your life is until I did not have one — good, bad or indifferent.

Many years later, my mom met a man who was God-sent. His name was Gilbert. It is just amazing how God knows what we need when we need it. This man loved life; he cherished every minute. I'll never forget the family vacations at Garner State Park going camping, horseback riding, rapids riding and dancing. This was truly the family I dreamed about. He was a spur-of-the-moment kind of person, and my mom was a perfectionist. She never wanted to leave anything undone. I can still hear my dad saying, "Joni, you can either stay home and get those dishes done, or we can go fishing, but there isn't enough time to do both." The house was always immaculate, and he knew it would not hurt her to leave a few dirty dishes. When dad said, "It's time to go," that meant he was in the car backing out.

He raced motocross at the Astrodome in Houston, Texas. He loved to ride motorcycles. He also liked to be in the crash-up derby contests. This man truly had a love for people and life. He did not have very many rules, but the ones he had, he expected you to obey. He also believed in working hard and being honest. My brother, Richard, really loved Gilbert. He hadn't had a dad figure in his life for a long time.

Every year, Gilbert would take us on vacation to my Aunt Linda's house outside of Corpus Christi at Weber's boat landing. That's where we would go fishing. I remember Richard and I getting in the canoe and rowing out to the middle of the lake to go cork fishing, and it started raining. I asked him, "Should we go in?" He said, "No, this is when the fish really start biting." My brother had the patience of Job when it came to fishing. He did not even have to get a bite all night. He just loved the idea of fishing. That day, I caught more fish than I ever caught in my life, and I have never caught that many fish since.

There was something about my aunt that I loved. She had peace and joy. My aunt did not hesitate to let you know how she felt and what she believed. My aunt is an awesome woman of God and she ministered to me by the way she lived her life. I was blessed with having someone to keep the prayer lines open.

Richard and I had so much fun when we were kids. When it flooded, we would make up all kinds of games. One was called *Jump the Ditch*. Our house sat right beside this ditch. The object was to jump this six-foot ditch without landing in it. I don't think I ever played this game without getting soaked. Also, in the summer months, Richard would take one side of the road and I would take the other, and we would look inside the meters for toads. We would collect as many as we could find, then return home to see who won.

Richard and I had a good relationship. I would always follow him around, and he would always tell me to stop it. I would tell on him every chance I got, and he did the same to me, but we loved each other. I remember walking down the street in the middle of summer talking to him, asking him all kinds of questions that I thought a big brother ought to know. Sometimes he would answer them, sometimes he would laugh, and sometimes he would tell me to be quiet. When we got into trouble, and that was most of the time, my mom believed in the "tattle-tale-and-consequences" method of punishment. If you told on someone, you got punished, and the person who did the crime got punished also. When this happened, we usually got grounded to our rooms, which worked out good for mom, but we sure were bored. The rooms were side by side with a big mirror hanging on the wall in between them. We used to make paper airplanes and throw them at each other in the mirror. We also liked to make spit balls and launch them at each other.

Richard liked to play jokes on people. One day, he went on a mission to find as many snakes as he could. When he came back to the house with a shirt full, he walked right into his room, pulled out his underwear drawer and placed the snakes in there as neatly as he could. Richard went back outside and waited for the moment that he could hear our mom scream.

My mom was doing laundry, and she headed back to Richard's room to put his shirts and socks away. She opened his underwear drawer, and you could have heard her from two states over. She yelled, "Richard Allen, get in this house right now!" That day, there was not a tattletale consequence. I don't think he ever did that again. Mom did not think that was funny at all. Years later, it is one of the funniest stories that she tells.

Back then, my mom took us to church. She loved the Lord. She wanted to raise her kids with Godly values. I remember my first experience in church. My mom would take us down the street to the local Methodist church. I don't think there was Sunday school, or if there was, my mom did not take us to it. I do know we had to be perfectly still, not a peep, or she would pinch us--not just a regular pinch, but a pinch with a twist. To be honest, we got our share of being pinched. As quiet as we had to be, there were a lot of seeds being planted in those years when we were in church. I have my mom to thank for that. Although the seeds would not be watered until much later in my life, they were always there. When I think about that, it is amazing to me how powerful our God is. The Scripture says: *He knows me and every hair on my head.* That alone is more than I could ask for, but He gave me so much more--more than I could hope for or dream I could have. Could you imagine the time it would take to know every hair on someone's head? God is faithful.

One night after my brother and I went to bed, we were awakened by a terrible noise. It sounded awful. We got up to see what had happened, and my mom was just sitting there crying. For the moment, everything just stood still. We knew it was bad, but we were not prepared for what was about to be unfolded. She began to tell us that our dad had been driving in his dune buggy with a friend. They had been drinking and driving on Galveston Bay wall. It was a steep wall, and everyone liked to ride motorcycles, bikes, and dune buggies on it. The wall was about a mile long. They decided to get a bottle and take a ride, but they approached the end sooner than they expected. Dad turned the buggy as sharply as he could. He did not want to go over because there was nothing down there but rocks and ocean. As soon as he turned it, it flipped over, breaking my dad's neck. He died instantly and his friend lived. I don't know why Gilbert had to die that night, but I do know, no matter what, God is faithful. God did not cause him to die. The lies of Satan did. I can hear Satan saying, "Oh, go ahead and drink and drive. Nothing will happen to you. People do it every day." God tells us many times throughout the Bible about obeying.

> *In Genesis 2:16, "And the Lord God commanded the man,*
> *"You are free to eat from any tree in the garden; but you*
> *must not eat from the tree of knowledge of good and evil,*
> *for when you eat of it you will surely die."" Acts 5:29 also*
> *says we must obey God rather than men.*

We shouldn't depend on man to know what we need. We need to learn to depend on God more and us less. I know if Gilbert had conformed into what the Lord wanted for him, he would have not been out on that wall driving under the influence. More often than not, we want to be the drivers in our own lives, and then we blame God for the wrecks we have created. I believe we need to be a people who want to serve the Lord, no matter what the cost; but every time we get a little nervous, or out of our comfort zone, we drive off.

The Lord said, *Keep your eyes focused on My kingdom and Me and everything else will be added unto you.* He came to give us an abundant life, not to kill us. Satan came to kill, steal, and destroy. That is how he works. He makes things look fun that are really dangerous and can kill you. Satan's goal is to kill you before you can find out the truth about the One who came to save you, Jesus. The One who gave His life so you could live.

After that night, everything changed. Where we once had security, we now had none. Our lives were left so empty. I remember when my softball coach came by to sign me up for the season. I just looked at him and said, "My dad died and my mom needs me this year. I won't be playing." I loved softball, but things were not going to be the same, and I knew that even as a small child. I'll never forget how my coach looked at me that day, and he said, "Maybe next year." His eyes were filled with sorrow. I will always remember his sweet spirit.

A year had gone by and our lives would never be the same. Richard was not handling Gilbert's death well at all, and he did not understand why he was taken from us. He had a lot of anger in him towards God and everyone around him. My brother really loved Gilbert. I could see the loss on Richard's face every time I looked at him. It was as if someone had stolen his smile only to replace it with tears of sorrow. It was as if my brother lost his only hope of being a part of a real family. The pain that penetrated his entire being was evident in his speech, his walk, his movement; his very soul yearned from a place I had never witnessed before in him. Mom started noticing a change when the school started calling about Richard getting into fights and not turning in his assignments.

It got worse, and he started hanging around the wrong people and doing the wrong things. Drugs became a part of his life, as well as alcohol, and he started smoking. He was getting into a lot more trouble. Our relationship was not the same; he did not want me around, and he started treating me with a lot of hostility.

I know my mother was getting concerned, so when my brother asked if he could go live with my real dad, even though she would have rather he stayed with her, she knew he needed to be around a father figure again, so she agreed.

I heard my mom make the phone call that night, and my brother was overjoyed. She knew, better than anyone, my dad had a bad temper and she warned Richard. Richard did not listen. That night, he thought mom was just trying to talk hatefully about our dad. I knew better. I still remembered that night he broke in. The place I had never witnessed in my brother before was an all too familiar place for me. I knew the pain of loss. I knew the pain of torment. I mourned my own purity of mind due to the things I witnessed as a small child. I could reveal truth to my brother, but was he in a place to receive? Would he be able to take another death, not of flesh and blood, but another death of his dreams of ever having a normal family? The answer to these questions, and to many more, will always remain a mystery because I never could bring myself to plead a case against his hope. I remained silent.

Chapter Two

Wisdom

The sun is shining; it is a new day . . .
Clouds fill my heart, only words left to say . . .
God give me the wisdom to understand . . .
My life is Your life, with only one plan . . .
I reach up to Heaven calling out Your Name . . .
Oh Lord, be with us through all this change...
Give me the heart to understand . . .
Give me the wisdom to know Your plan . . .

It was just my mom and I now, and I could tell she was really lonely and afraid of being without Gilbert. It had been a little over a year and she had started dating. I do not think it was because she was ready, but I don't think she liked being alone. The change in her had come little by little. I started noticing it after she started dating this man. Although he was sweet on the outside, his insides were "tore up from the floor up." He had a very cruel side, which we would learn about later. They dated a few months, and then decided to get married. The memories of Gilbert filled our house, and he wanted us to start a new life with him, so he suggested we move. Plus, he had a lot of money, and I'm sure he wanted a bigger house. So we moved to another house and began our life with this new man, another stepdad for me. At first, our lives seemed good. We had plenty of money and friends. I was popular at school. I played a lot of sports, such as volleyball and basketball, and I was on the track team. All the teachers liked me. Things were good for a while.

I started noticing that there was something strange about my stepdad. He had a weird side to him. My mom did not seem very happy. I think she realized that she got married too fast after Gilbert's death, but she was lonely and thought that my stepdad could fill that void for her. My mother started seeing a psychiatrist every week, but she just wasn't getting any better. I did not understand how this was happening. Later, I found out that my stepdad was behind it. He was slowly increasing my mom's medication to get her to do some things she normally would not do. He was sick.

Before long, my mom was in a bad way. She really did not know what was going on most of the time. I don't know if he was blackmailing her somehow to stay with him. I am not sure, but I knew that my mother had changed in a significant way. It did not take long for our house to be known as the party house. To see my mom so out of it on drugs bothered me. She was who I counted on, and I was losing her due to the choices she was making. The loneliness I felt was unbearable. I went to school and tried to act like everything was great, but everyone knew better. They had seen my mom and stepdad, and they knew everything was far from being great. Things started to get worse. I think my mom wanted to divorce him. He had my mom committed.

I remember talking to my stepdad one time, and I mentioned that I was scared of bugs, especially June bugs. He took a real interest in the things I feared. One night as I was getting ready for bed, I shut my door and pulled back the covers. When I did, I saw a lot of June bugs crawling all over my bed. I screamed and cried. I could not believe he did this to me. I could not imagine what entered his mind to make him do such a thing to a child. I wondered what he was thinking when he was collecting all those bugs. Was he thinking how funny it was going to be, or was he thinking how scared I would be, or was he just not thinking. I can tell you this, if you do not have the Lord on your mind and in your heart, Satan can get in. The Bible says, *You are either for Me or you are against Me*. It is that simple.

I don't know how long my mom was in the mental hospital, but I do remember visiting her. I wondered why she was there, because she did not act like the other people that I had seen there. I knew that my stepdad was behind all of this, but I could not prove it. My mom came home and everything was back to normal.

One evening, the phone rang and it was Rhonda, a friend I used to hang around with when my dad was alive. She wanted to know if I could go with her and another friend to an amusement park. I asked my mom and she said sure. The next morning, my friend's mom came and got me to take us to the park. It took about 30 minutes to get there. She was going to drop us off and pick us up at closing.

We were so excited to be going to this park. When we got there, we paid for our tickets, and I remember making the comment that I wished I had a season pass so I could go anytime I wanted. My friend had one and so did our other friend. We went into the amusement park, and we headed straight for the roller coasters. We rode them for a while and decided to go to the other side of the park. As we were walking, I noticed that a man was following us. I told my friend to watch and see if she thought someone was following us. We would walk into stores, look around, and when we would come out, he would be there. Everywhere we went, he was there. We were only 11 and did not know what to do about it, so we stopped and told the security guard. He said he knew him. He was a police officer. So we decided to go ride some more rides and forget about it. A couple of hours went by, and finally, the man approached us. He wanted to know if we wanted to help catch some bad guys. He showed us his badge, and he assured us that it was okay with our parents; he said he already called them. He also said that if we helped them catch these guys, they would give us one thousand dollars. Rhonda and our other friend thought about it and said no. I was still thinking about it when he also offered a free season pass. I stood there for a few moments and then decided to help. The police officer told Rhonda and our friend to go ride the rides, and we would all meet back there about 5:00 p.m. As I watched them walk away, I was so excited about helping out and getting paid with a season pass, that I did not bother to ask what I would be doing. Moments later, the police officer asked what my address and phone number were.

I was puzzled. I said, "You told me you already talked to my mom and she said it was okay for me to help you." He said, "Oh, I know, I am just confirming so I know where to send the check to," and that sounded okay to me. I was only eleven.

We started walking around almost like we were trying to find someone. Every now and again, he would go and talk to a security guard. He told me they were working with him, and he was checking on information. He seemed really secretive and that scared me. I remember the police officer walking me to a bench and telling me not to move; he had people watching me. He was going to go in the store, and he would be right back. It seems like it took forever, but he came back with a paper bag and a coke. He sat down and offered me a drink. I took a drink of it, and it had a funny taste to it. I was starting to have doubts about what was going to happen. I set the coke on the edge of the bench so it would spill. When it did, he got really upset with me. Then he told me to get up. He said we needed to walk around so his helpers could get a good look at me, so they would know that I was one of the good guys. He was good. He kept me believing that I was really helping the police. Finally, we approached this place that had been abandoned. The attraction had not been working for months. We went across the bars, through some trees and down towards a ditch about 6 feet deep.

The police officer told me to sit down on my knees. He was looking all around from one side to the other. I asked him what he was doing. He said making sure they could see us. I asked, "Who?" He said, "The people we were helping." Then he opened the bag and pulled out a rope. I just looked at him. He told me what he was going to do. He said he was going to tie my hands behind my back and not to say a word. I knew in this very moment, I was going to become another statistic. For the next hour, this man used my body for his pleasure. Then he whispered in my ear, "I am going to leave now. You count to 100 and then you can leave." 1-2-3-4-5-6-7-8-9 all the way until I reached one hundred.

As I was kneeling, I realized God had saved me. He was the One untying me. I got up and went looking for this man, but the park was closed. I was determined to find him. Why? For the season pass - *the faith of a child.* I still believed in some sick way, I was helping the police. It would not be until later that I realized what happened to me. The place was really dark, and I was having trouble finding my way to the front gates. It seemed like it took me forever to get where I needed to be. Finally seeing some light, I heard a woman screaming, "Where is she? What has happened to her? Are you going to go look for her?" As I got closer, I realized it was my friend's mom. They were standing there with this awful look on their faces, crying and crying. I thought they were upset at me for being late.

After some paperwork, and after I told them what happened to me, I think they offered me a season pass. They did not want any unnecessary attention. It would cause panic and certainly was not good for business. I passed on the season pass. It no longer appealed to me. It no longer held the same value as it once did. The place where I went to have fun and be free with my friends, and escape some of my pain, now was a part of my pain. I found myself with no place to hide, no place to feel safe, no place to escape the reality of my life.

They took me home and explained to my mom what had happened. I went to take the longest shower I'd ever taken and cried as many tears as I could bear to cry. I had never felt as dirty as I did that day. I still did not understand really what happened to me. It went through my mind about a thousand times—what I could have done to change what had happened. My mother made me an appointment with a psychiatrist. When I was introduced to him, all I could think was, *Great, another man. What is he going to do that the others have not already done? What is left of my purity? What is left of my self-worth?* My trust in men, by this point, was dissipating. I went to him for a while, but I do not think it helped me. He was just another stranger in my world of confusion. My mom and I did not talk about it; it hurt my mom too much. Holding it all in sure had its problems later in life for me. Only God knows how I struggled with the pain. I could not stand to be touched by most men for a long time, especially older men. I always thought someone was watching me, and I had a lot of fear. I based many of my decisions on the fear—the fear of never being able to trust again.

I had nightmares every night. All I could think about was that this man had my address and phone number. He could come get me if they didn't catch him. Weeks went by. I could hardly keep my mind on anything. I was always looking over my shoulder. One day, the phone rang and it was the police. They said they had caught him. I was so relieved. Although the memories of him were horrible, at least I didn't have to be scared that he was going to find me and kill me. The police also said that I was really lucky to be alive that day at the park because this man did this all over the place. Sometimes, he would masquerade as a police officer, like he did with me, or sometimes, he would masquerade as a superintendent of a school.

The next few months were very hard. I had gone back to school trying to catch up on some of my work. The harder I tried, the worse I felt. I just could not function right. I felt like everyone knew, and they were looking at me. I felt as if I should be wearing a sign "Innocence gone. Purity has passed away." I also felt so stupid for believing that man. Every time I looked in the mirror, I could see him. He was overweight and had a wide nose. He wore his hair parted on the right side. He had fat hands. I noticed his hands because I believe I saw a wedding ring; and he was short. I could not take enough showers, and I never did feel clean, no matter what I did or how many showers I took. My mind did not seem right. Even when I was awake, I would close my eyes and he would be there just staring at me. The things he did to me literally made me sick to my stomach.

One day when I got home, the phone rang. It was the same officer who called when they caught him. He asked to talk to my mom. All I could hear was her saying, "Okay, how did this happen?" When she got off the phone, she was crying. She said, "Sit down, Michele. I have something to tell you. Remember when they called and said that they had caught him? Well, he escaped last night." Then she went on to tell me that the officer said this man was highly intelligent. He had escaped many times. He had even jumped from a helicopter once, but the officer assured my mom he would be caught again. I went hysterical. I could not believe this was happening. I remember asking God, *"Why? Why should this man be free? Why should I live in fear of the unknown? Why was my purity taken and then replaced with the fear of death?"* Many years later after being taught the Word of God, I realized we live in a world with Satan, and just as God has a plan for our lives, so does Satan. He has come to destroy us, and he will use any means to accomplish his purpose, including molesting a child of God.

My mom thought it would be good for me to have a friend over to spend the night, so I invited someone. We were just goofing off, having a good time calling my mom. We had two different phone lines in the house. We would call her and say we want a coke or some chips, and she would laugh. The music was playing loudly. We were dancing, and my phone rang. I picked it up, and I heard a voice say, "I'm watching you, I know what you're wearing and I'm coming to get you." Then the phone went dead. I just stood there. My legs felt like rubber. I could not move.

My friend said, "Who was that on the phone," but before I could answer her, I heard a noise outside my window. It was the bushes, scraping back and forth. I started screaming, and then my friend started screaming. I flew out of my room and there stood my stepdad, laughing and laughing. My mom came running from the other side of the house, and I told her what had happened. She could not believe his sick mind.

A couple of years had passed, and I was in my early teens. I was starting to like boys, and I found one who I thought was a nice guy.

He went to my school, and his parents were pleasant. We started dating, if you can call it that. We went to the movies together. Our parents would drop us off and pick us up after the movie was over. We held hands to our classroom, and I guess you could say we were going steady. We were just like any other teenagers going steady. We broke up and got back together. We went steady off and on for at least a year. I thought I loved him. He was my first kiss, first boyfriend, and first date.

He was a nice guy, but somehow he got involved with drugs. He didn't just do a little here and there, and he did not start out slow. Within months, he was doing drugs all the time and mostly at my house. His parents would come over looking for him a lot. They would drag him out of our house. He was not getting the drugs there at this time, but eventually, he would. I tried to tell him that it was changing him, but his desire to get high all the time overwhelmed him. At times, I think he really wanted to stop, but he did not know how. His mom and dad put him into drug rehab, and he would do well for a while, until he would get out and get around some of his old friends. Our relationship did not last. The drugs were too important, and we were way too young to be getting so involved; but I thought I was in love with him.

My stepdad and mom were not getting along, and my mom could not take any more of him or his perversion. A few months later, my mom filed for a divorce. Another chapter in my life closed, only to open a more terrifying one. What lay ahead was usually only seen in a fiction movie... unless you were living my life.

Michele Davenport

Michele's second excerpt is from her poetry book called *From My Heart to Yours Devotional*. In it, Michele offers a glimpse of Scriptural commentary as she intertwines her own poetry with the Word of God. It's a must read devotional, perfect for a morning Bible study.

From My Heart to Yours Devotional

Lori Michele Davenport

From My Heart to Yours

I have given you love and forgiveness, through my grace,
All that I ask is you seek My face.
Remember Me when the times get rough,
Be secure in knowing that I am enough.

When my Son rises in the righteous ones,
The healing in Their wings has begun.
You are being strengthened with every passing day,
The bridge between us is our escape.

Built in an arch that covers our sin,
From the flowing waters where you have been.

Cast in the sea without a thought,
My Son has been given; your sins have been bought.

He paid the price, the final cost,
He saved your soul from being lost.

Now I live in you, and you live in Me,
This is My creation, the way I created you to be.

Ephesians 1:7-8,

"In Him we have redemption through His blood, the forgiveness of sins, in accordance with the riches of God's grace that He lavished on us with all wisdom and understanding."

Now let's look at the word redemption, *"apotutrosis:* ransom in full, something to loosen (Strong's #629 Gk.)"

God paid the price for us with His Son's blood. God has already loosed us from the hold of the enemy. Why do we keep trying to repay a debt that is paid in full? Would you send a payment on a bill you did not owe? God's grace is sufficient; it is our lack of understanding that keeps us from all that God has to offer.

What debt are you always trying to pay? Why do you feel the need to pay it?

_____

_____

_____

_____

<u>Rekindle Your Spirit</u>

Are you consumed with all of the tomorrows,
That you are ungrateful for today?

Caught up in this life,
Forgetting the need to pray.
I wonder when you're alone,
Do you realize your Life is not your own.

I am between the silences, in the night,
Fighting to show you the plans I have made for your life,

The things you're saving for will soon fade away,
Lay your treasures up in heaven where they are safe.
The day is short, with limited time,
The seasons are passing with My signs.

Rekindle your spirit then connect it with Mine.
It's not too late, I have saved the time.

Psalms 119:36-40,

"Turn my heart towards your statutes and not towards selfish gain. Turn my eyes away from worthless things; preserve my life according to your word. Fulfill your promise to your servant, so that you may be feared. Take away the disgrace I dread, for your laws are good. How I long for your precepts! Preserve my life in your righteousness."

"Precepts" is a very interesting word in Hebrew. It is *"pigguwd,"* meaning "mandate, appointed, authorization (Strong's #6490)." God has already authorized power to be given to us; we just need to receive the power. Our main problem is a receiving problem rather than a giving problem.

When is the last time you asked God for a healing? Did you know the healing was already yours; all you needed to do was receive it? Can you really believe? Can you put your faith in the Word? God sent the Word and turned it into flesh (Jesus).

_____

_____

_____

_____

<u>Captives Free</u>

Watching the sins of my life,
As they're being deleted from Your sight.

The wrong I have done, has been washed by your Son,
Now I have my chance, I have begun.

You had chosen me before I was born,
Ripped from this world battered and torn.

You spoke to my heart, and made me whole,
Then placed Your candle in the midst of my soul.

The fire that burns is my spirit within,
To know You more, to be Your friend.

My memories fade far from the pain,
The desires of my heart are not the same.

Remaining still while life passes by,
Watching Your people while they live to die.

Carelessly counting the souls unseen,
Not questioning what they believe.

Being content with my safe place,
No mercy they find not knowing Your grace.

Oh Lord, give me wisdom a vision to see,
When Your Word leaves my mouth, set them free.

Galatians 5:1,

"Stand fast therefore in the liberty wherewith Christ hath made us free, and be not entangled again with the yoke of bondage."

Bondage: *"douleuo*-slavery (Strong's #1397 Gk)." When the enemy tries to constantly remind you of your past mistakes, he is trying to keep you a slave to guilt. If he can keep your focus on your past, then he can keep *his* focus on your future. Repent and go on.

Think about who you are holding in prison with your own unforgiveness. Write it down, forgive them, and then be forgiven yourself. Who holds the keys to your prison?

_____

_____

_____

_____

The third book, *"Choices are for the Living,"* a teaching book perhaps, but far more than teaching, it challenges the readers to ask themselves one profound question, "Do I fear the Lord?" It forces the readers to look in the mirror of self and reexamine their motives and beliefs, by making them realize their choices speak loudly about what they really believe.

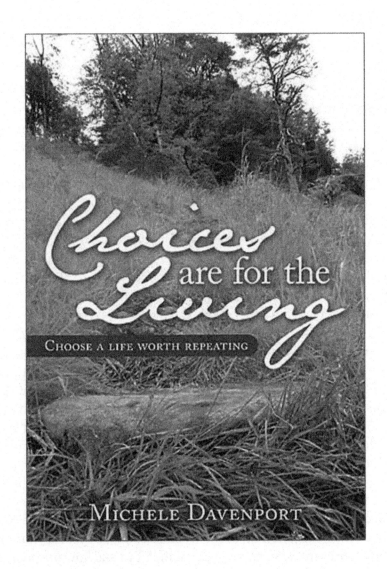

Choices are for the Living

CHOOSE A LIFE WORTH REPEATING

MICHELE DAVENPORT

Introduction

Choices are for the living and the choices we make are made many times out of our emotions, opinions, and life experiences, not necessarily out of the fear of the Lord. What does it mean to fear God? What does that even look like to you? Could it mean to tremble every time you sin? Could it mean shaking when His Name is spoken aloud? Or could it possibly mean reading His Word and then doing His Word, according to His Word. Examine the Scriptures for yourself and let them reveal His truth. The word "fear" is written in the NKJV Bible 367 times, and of those 367 times, 118 times are associated in direct fear of the Lord. I wrote this book, not because I have arrived in any way, shape or form at understanding the fear of the Lord, but because I believe it has been misunderstood, and therefore, ignored. If I could, I would take out the 51 times in the NKJV Scriptures that said, *"Do not fear."* It would make my goal a lot easier if the Bible did not appear to contradict itself. **"Do not fear,"** then **"fear"** sounds a bit contrary to the Word. We must distinguish between the two fears; "Do not fear" means "do not fear for I am with you," as it is written in Isaiah 41:10 (NIV). Hebrews 11:7 (NIV) says, "By faith Noah, being warned by God concerning events as yet unseen, in reverent fear constructed an ark for the saving of his household. By this he condemned the world and became an heir of the righteousness that comes by faith." The fear of the Lord actually saved mankind; the whole human race was saved because Noah took God at His Word. God said build an ark and Noah grabbed the nails and went to the wood pile. So, as I journey through the Scriptures to discover the Word of the Lord and how my own fear of Him establishes who I am, I invite you on my journey to discover for yourself the importance of acknowledging the Scriptures.

*As you are reading my book I will be referencing the NIV, ESV, and the Message Bible and will provide a list in the appendix of all resources.

<u>**Chapter 1**</u>

I don't want to be on the left side...

Proverbs 1:7, "The fear of the Lord is the beginning of knowledge; fools despise wisdom and instruction."

Fearing the Lord is not something we're into as humans and believers of the Gospel. As a matter of fact, many believers don't understand the fear of the Lord at all. On one hand, many think the fear of the Lord is quivering every time we make a mistake. The reason I decided to write a book on the subject is not that I understand the fear of the Lord to my full capability, or even to yours, but I believe as I am faithful to write, the Holy Spirit will be faithful to teach. I have been a Christian for over twenty years and I have never heard anyone say these words, "I woke up today in great fear of the Lord." We love to infatuate ourselves with His promises, His grace, and His mercy, but when it comes to fearing Him, we quickly quote the 51 times the Scriptures say, "Do not fear," and then ignore the 118 times the Scriptures demand us to be in utter awe and fear of the Lord. We can't get out our kindergarten box of crayons and color God in the image our minds can relate to, nor can we adopt the God of our parents, or even who our church says God is. We need to pick up the Word and read it for ourselves to see who we believe God is. Who is God to you? Stop and think it about it for a moment.

We have become nothing more than people pleasers instead of God pleasers. We fear people, situations and statistics more than God. Here are some interesting facts. The Sunday supplement magazine, "USA Weekend," ran a cover story entitled "Fear: What Americans

Are Afraid of Today." In a scientific poll, the magazine uncovered the things Americans fear most:

> 54 % are "afraid" or "very afraid" of being in a car crash.
> 53 % are "afraid" or "very afraid" of having cancer.
> 50 % are "afraid" or "very afraid" of inadequate Social Security.
> 49% are "afraid" or "very afraid" of not having enough money for retirement.
> 36 % are "afraid" or "very afraid" of food poisoning from meat.
> 35 % are "afraid" or "very afraid' of getting Alzheimer's.
> 34 % are "afraid" or "very afraid" of pesticides on food.
> 33% are "afraid" or "very afraid" of being a victim of an individual violence.
> 32% are "afraid" or "very afraid" of being unable to pay current debts.
> 30% are "afraid" or "very afraid" of exposure to foreign viruses.
> 28 % are "afraid" or "very afraid" of getting Aids.
> 25% are "afraid" or "very afraid" of natural disasters.

After I finished reading this, I quickly realized it appeared Americans did not fear God at all. One of the largest fears in America is being in a car crash. I thought about finding out the statistics on all of the fears and seeing if it was even rational to be fearful of these things, but I decided that was not what this book is about. This book is about fearing God, the Creator of the Universe. It is not about if you should fear those other things, but rather why many of us don't feel it necessary to fear God. Isaiah 66:2 says, "But this is the one to whom I will look: he who is humble and contrite in spirit and trembles at my word." Let me ask you a question, do you tremble at God's Word?

How do you respond to Matthew 25:34-46, "Then the King will say to those on his right side, 'Come, you who are blessed by my Father, inherit the kingdom prepared for you from the foundation of the world. For I was hungry and you gave me food, I was thirsty and you gave me drink, I was a stranger and you welcomed me, I was naked *and you clothed me, I was sick and you visited me, I was in prison and you came to me.' Then the righteous will answer him, saying, 'Lord when did we see you sick or in prison and visit you?' And the King will answer them, 'Truly, I say to you, as you did it to one of the least of these my brothers, you did it to me.' Then he will **say to those on the left**, 'Depart from me, you cursed, into the eternal fire prepared for the devil and his angels. For I was hungry and you gave me no food, I was thirsty and you gave me no drink, I was a stranger and you did not welcome me, naked and you did not clothe me, sick and in prison and you did not visit me.' Then they also will answer, saying, 'Lord, when did we see you hungry or thirsty or a stranger or naked or sick or in prison, and did not minister to you?' Then he will answer them, saying, 'Truly, I say to you, as you did not do it to one of the least of these, you did not do it to me.' And these will go away into eternal punishment, but the righteous into eternal life."*

Do you look at Matthew 25:34-46 as if these Scriptures apply to everyone else? If you really trembled at His Word, you could not look at these Scriptures and ignore the value of them. You could no longer pass by a man hungry on the side of the road only to get yourself to the other side, or flip the channel when hungry children from Africa come on because it's uncomfortable for you to watch. After reading and teaching several Bible Studies on *Remembering the Forgotten God*, by Francis Chan, I was challenged to live even more accurately according to God's Word. Years before I heard of Francis Chan, I had a heart for the needy in every aspect of the word. I was the lady who held up traffic to give someone a meal. Or if I saw someone on the side of the road in need of prayer, I would stop to pray. I have a tender heart for God's people and I hold myself accountable to His Word. As I taught his Bible study, I grew deeper in the Lord, right along with the ladies taking the class, because "What you have done for the least of these you have done unto me." I had made up my mind to quit playing church like it was an instrument I could pick up and put down at my leisure, and start being the church. To be an instrument that God could use. Have you ever bought a second-hand piano or guitar? Usually when you buy an instrument second-hand, it will need some tuning. Well church, how long will we sit up in the balcony applauding the orchestra and being in awe of the conductor?

How long will we just sit in the repair shop, waiting for "church," to be tuned, fixed, restored, pampered and babied before we start living an accurate life according to God's Word?

We are the church, so if we are upset with how things are happening in the church, we should be upset with ourselves. We have all allowed the mimicking, pretending, and the putting on airs; we not only allow it, we are doing it as well. Believers, we are so far off from where the church originated from in the book of Acts. The churches today remind me of the type of house my family and I used to live in, in Texas. The houses were called "cookie cutter" homes. They only took about three months to build. It took longer to go through the paperwork to buy the house than it did to build it. The reason they were called cookie cutter homes was the builder would offer several different floor plans to choose from, but they were all made out of basically the same material, constructed by the same builder, painted by the same painters, bricked by the same brick layers. In other words, the floor plans were a little different, but the houses were more or less the same. This is what I think happened to the local body of Christ. We have made cookie cutter churches. We have used the architect and blueprints of the churches around us, instead of the original architect of the book of Acts.

In Hebrews 11:10 the Scripture says, "For he was looking forward to the city that has foundations, whose designer and builder is God." Sure the churches look a little different on the inside-different music, different programs, different styles of preaching, but basically the same. Nowhere do I find the church of today in the blueprint of Acts. We have strayed from the original plan of God's church for those whose designers and builders are men and not God. I think many pastors have made being a pastor more of a job than a calling. Is the church accurately living Matthew 25:34-46 ?

Let's reflect again on Matthew 25:40 which says, "And the King will answer them, Truly, I say to you, as you did it to one of the least of these my brothers, you did it to me." Wow!!! You know this means good or bad. Every time we choose to ignore the hurting world around us, we have done this unto Him. Every time we sit around getting fat and happy while investing our money for our future only, instead of investing in a life worth saving, we have done this unto Him. Every time we store our riches up on earth, while ignoring the kingdom of God, we have done this unto Him. Every time we care more about things than people, we have done this unto Him. I am telling you, I understand it like never before. Ever since I taught on *Remembering the Forgotten God* by Francis Chan, the flashlight which I allowed the Holy Spirit to lead me by has turned into a floodlight. I am in this thing with my eyes wide open and my ears fully awake.

Many of us have developed a "no tolerance" policy. We see the hungry man standing on the side of the road, and we turn our nose up as if to say as flippantly as we can, "A man doesn't work, a man doesn't eat." Who are you to judge who eats and who doesn't?

Do you know the man or woman standing on the side of the road? Do you know their situation? Do you know for a fact that they are just being lazy, that they had a job and just up and quit so they could come stand on a street corner and hold up a sign begging for food? My guess would be no, you don't. I would rather stand before my God having fed the hungry than to stand before my God and say something stupid like, "Well I thought they needed to work to eat so I let them go hungry." I decided who ate and who didn't; that was my job. 1 John 4:20-21 says, "For if anyone says, 'I love God,' and hates his brother, he is liar; for he who does not love his brother whom he has seen cannot love God whom he has not seen. And this commandment we have from him: whoever loves God must also love his brother." Your brother is considered to be the one you don't know, maybe someone you have never even seen. "Whatever you did for one of the least of these brothers of mine, you did for me." Have you become a liar? Do you say you love Jesus but ignore the hurting people who surround you every day? If Jesus came back today, what would He find you doing?

Choices are for the Living:

1. Are you on the right side or left side at this moment in your life?

_____

_____

_____

2. What are you most afraid of and why? Do you fear the Lord?

_____

_____

_____

3. What is the first thing you think of when you think of fearing the Lord?

_____

_____

_____

4. Who is the Lord to you?

_____

_____

_____

_____

5. When was the last time you fed a hungry person?

_____

_____

_____

_____

Weekly challenge: Give 5% of your weekly income to your favorite charity, and while there, volunteer.

Additional Notes:

_____

_____

_____

_____

_____

Michele speaks at churches and women's retreats and teaches regularly. To contact the author, you can email her at fbmin02@gmail.com, or to order her other books, go to her web page at fbministries.com.

CPSIA information can be obtained
at www.ICGtesting.com
Printed in the USA
BVOW04*0759010617
485567BV00007B/5/P